Hidden Europe - Small cities and towns that are off the beaten path

By Jack Howard

Introduction

Welcome to an enchanting journey through the lesser-known destinations of Europe, where the essence of charm and allure thrives in the embrace of small cities and towns. While the grandeur of famous capitals often steals the spotlight, it is in these hidden gems that the true heart and soul of Europe can be found.

This book invites you to traverse the cobblestone streets, meandering alleyways, and picturesque squares that define the very fabric of these remarkable places. Through the pages that follow, we will delve into the captivating stories, unique cultures, and enticing attractions that make these hidden gems a treasure trove for travelers seeking an authentic European experience.

From the sun-kissed shores of the Adriatic to the misty highlands of Scotland, each chapter will unravel the secrets of a specific European destination. Join us as we uncover the hidden histories, vibrant local traditions, and extraordinary natural landscapes that set these small cities and towns apart from their more renowned counterparts.

As you embark on this literary adventure, prepare to be immersed in the distinctive charm and unpretentious beauty that characterize these lesser-explored destinations. Get ready to unlock the mysteries behind their ancient architecture, sample the flavors of their traditional cuisines, and discover the hidden gems that lie off the beaten path.

Whether you are an intrepid explorer, a passionate history enthusiast, or simply seek an escape from the bustling city life, this book will serve as your invaluable companion. Embrace the thrill of venturing into the lesser-trodden corners of Europe and let yourself be captivated by the allure of small cities and towns.

So, grab your suitcase, pack your curiosity, and embark on the journey of a lifetime. The hidden gems of Europe eagerly await your discovery, and with every page turned, you will find yourself falling deeper under their irresistible spell.

Welcome to a world where enchantment lies just around the corner, in the hidden nooks and crannies of Europe's small cities and towns. Let us embark on this exploration together and uncover the profound charm that resides off the beaten path.

How to Travel the Less Traveled in Europe

As the world becomes increasingly connected, travelers are seeking new and authentic experiences beyond the well-trodden tourist paths. While popular destinations such as Paris, Rome, and London will always attract their share of visitors, there is something deeply rewarding about discovering the lesser-known gems tucked away amid the diverse landscapes of Europe. In this chapter, we explore how to travel the less traveled in Europe and embrace a journey into the heart of authenticity.

Venture off the beaten track

Instead of flocking to popular cities and attractions, consider exploring smaller towns and rural regions that remain sheltered from mass tourism. From medieval villages perched atop cliffs in Italy to picturesque hamlets hidden within lush valleys or ancient ruins nestled among rolling hills, these lesser-known destinations provide travelers with an intimate look into authentic European life. Research lesser-known attractions in each country or region you plan to visit and prioritize these locations over a typical tourist itinerary.

Slow travel

Rather than racing from one city or monument to another, embrace the concept of slow travel and immerse yourself in your surroundings. This involves staying longer at each destination, allowing you ample time to understand its unique culture and history while forming genuine connections with locals. Participate in activities such as wine tasting, traditional cooking classes, or village festivals; these charming experiences will leave you with fond memories and a deeper appreciation for your destination's cultural fabric.

Choose local accommodations

Bypass chain hotels and consider staying in locally owned establishments like family-run bed-and-breakfasts, cozy farmhouses, or even native homestays. These local accommodations often provide a more intimate atmosphere and allow for greater engagement with your hosts, thus enriching your overall travel experience.

Utilize public transport

Relying on public transportation offers wonderful opportunities for interacting with locals and witnessing authentic scenes of daily life. Whether it's hopping on a bus that winds its way through quaint villages or boarding a regional train to traverse scenic countryside landscapes, public transport will add a unique dimension to your European adventure.

Indulge in local cuisine

European cuisine is as diverse as its landscapes, and there is no better way to truly appreciate a culture than by indulging in its culinary delights. Visit local markets where you can sample fresh produce and regional specialties while supporting small-scale food vendors.

Embrace culinary exploration by trying dishes exclusive to the area, seek out local eateries where residents gather, and don't hesitate to ask locals for recommendations – they know the best spots!

Learn the language

Even learning basic phrases in the local language can open doors for conversation and connection with residents. Make it a point to learn greetings, pleasantries, or even how to order food in each country you visit. Locals will appreciate your effort and be more inclined to engage in conversations, providing you with invaluable insights into their culture and way of life.

Travel outside peak season

By visiting Europe during shoulder or off-peak seasons, not only will you avoid the throngs of tourists but also be treated to a more authentic experience. Local residents are typically friendlier during less busy times and are more likely to interact with visitors.

By following these seven guidelines, you'll uncover unique moments far removed from conventional travel destinations, bringing you closer to what makes Europe so intoxicating – its people, culture, and tradition. So grab your backpack or suitcase, step off the beaten track, and embark on an adventure into the heart of an undiscovered Europe.

Western Europe

Aberdeen, Scotland

Located on the northeast coast of Scotland, Aberdeen is a city steeped in history, culture, and natural beauty. Known as the Granite City because of its numerous gray stone buildings, Aberdeen is both an architectural gem and a vibrant destination for travelers seeking a unique Scottish experience.

Upon arrival in Aberdeen, visitors are immediately struck by the city's impressive skyline. Dotted with medieval towers, churches, and historical landmarks standing proudly beside sleek modern structures, the city offers a striking contrast between old and new.

One iconic site that should not be missed on any visit to Aberdeen is the beautiful St. Machar Cathedral. Established in 1136 AD, this stunning Gothic structure houses numerous significant historical artifacts, including a well-preserved wooden archway from the 15th century.

History enthusiasts will also enjoy exploring Old Aberdeen - a veritable treasure trove of ancient buildings and narrow cobbled streets that transports visitors back in time. Key attractions include King's College, the residence of early Scottish monarchs; and Provost Skene's House, a well-preserved example of a 16th-century townhouse.

For those who prefer nature to architecture, there are plenty of outdoor activities to enjoy around Aberdeen. The dramatic coastline offers breathtaking views of rugged cliffs and the perfect opportunity to spot marine life such as dolphins and seals. Meanwhile, inland you'll find lush green parks such as Duthie Park and Hazlehead Park where visitors can wander among flower beds or enjoy leisurely picnics.

The wider Aberdeenshire area is renowned for its whiskey production, boasting more than 50 distilleries within driving distance from the city. Connoisseurs can embark on excursions to sample some of Scotland's finest single malts while learning about the art of whiskey-making during guided tours at iconic distilleries like Glenfiddich or Glenlivet.

When it comes to dining, Aberdeen offers an array of options to suit any taste – from traditional Scottish fare to contemporary international cuisine. Seafood lovers cannot miss the opportunity to try freshly caught fish and shellfish at one of the city's numerous local bistros or upscale restaurants, while those with a sweet tooth will revel in the mouth-watering selection of desserts available – with Scottish tablet (a dense tablet-like fudge) being a local specialty.

Aberdeen is well connected to other major cities in Scotland and the UK, making it easy for travelers to incorporate it into their itinerary. The city benefits from regular train and bus services, while the international airport serves numerous major European destinations.

Accommodation options in Aberdeen range from budget-friendly hostels to luxury hotels. Numerous bed and breakfast establishments or self-catering apartments provide a cozy home-away-from-home experience while allowing visitors to immerse themselves in local life.

Throughout the year, Aberdeen hosts a diverse array of cultural events and festivals that cater to all interests – from food and drink expos to literary gatherings and music concerts. A highlight on the annual calendar is the Aberdeen International Youth Festival – a multicultural celebration that showcases young talents from Scotland and beyond in the realms of dance, theater, music, and more.

Aberdeen presents endless opportunities for exploration and enjoyment during your visit. Whether you're fascinated by history, appreciate fine whiskey or prefer natural splendors, you'll be captivated by what this charming city on Scotland's northeastern coast has to offer. So why not start planning your trip today? Be sure not only to prepare your camera but also your senses for this memorable journey.

Marvão, Portugal

Imagine standing atop a rugged mountain with the entire world spread out below you, the sky an endless blue canvas that stretches as far as your eyes can see. This is the enchanting experience that awaits you when you visit Marvão, Portugal's timeless hilltop treasure.

Perched on a granite crag at an altitude of 2,800 feet, the small medieval village of Marvão offers breathtaking panoramic vistas of the surrounding Alentejo region. Cobblestone streets wind their way up to the remarkable 13th-century castle, while whitewashed houses with terracotta roofs nestle against each other, creating a perfect blend of natural beauty and architectural prowess.

Your journey to Marvão can begin in Lisbon or Faro; both airports are approximately three hours away by car. As you drive through the rolling hills and vast plains of Alentejo, be prepared to be enchanted by olive groves, vineyards, and cork oak forests on your approach to this magical land. The anticipation builds until you catch sight of the village looming majestically over its surroundings.

Upon arrival in Marvão, allow yourself time to wander through the narrow streets and soak up the village's history which dates back to pre-Roman times. Visit gothic treasures like Igreja do Espírito Santo and Convento de Nossa Senhora da Estrela as well as picturesque nooks punctuated by blooming flowers.

No exploration of Marvão would be complete without a visit to its crowning jewel: the Castle of Marvão. Constructed in 1299 under King Dinis I, this fortified marvel features a stunning keep and ramparts that provide an awe-inspiring view. Traverse the battlements while imagining ancient battles and intrigues once played out within these formidable walls.

Marvão isn't just about the past; it has plenty to offer the modern traveler. As you stroll through the village, stop by local shops selling artisanal products like ceramics, jewelry, and regional delicacies. Sample award-winning wine and indulge in authentic Alentejo cuisine at one of Marvão's fine restaurants.

When the sun sets, experience a night beneath the stars in charming accommodations ranging from sophisticated hotels to quaint guesthouses. The choice is yours as to whether you stay within Marvão's historic walls or venture out into the peaceful countryside that surrounds the village.

No visit to Marvão is complete without exploring the great outdoors. The surrounding landscape provides ample opportunity for hiking, mountain biking, and birdwatching. Venture into the Natural Park of Serra de São Mamede and marvel at its diverse flora and fauna. Along an array of walking trails, you might even stumble upon ancient stone menhirs or dolmens.

Marvão isn't just a holiday destination; it's a window into a forgotten age when knights defended their lands with sword and shield. It's also an opportunity to lose yourself in the simple pleasure of a leisurely walk through centuries-old streets without a care in the world.

As you say goodbye to this enchanted mountaintop village, you'll carry with you memories of panoramic vistas, ancient architecture, and warm sunsets that will linger in your heart long after you've returned home.

Monschau, Germany

Located in the heart of the Eifel region in western Germany, the charming town of Monschau enchants its visitors with its 500-year-old half-timbered houses, winding cobblestone streets, and idyllic landscapes. Visiting Monschau is like stepping back in time, and it offers a unique and unforgettable experience for travelers and history enthusiasts alike.

Arriving in Monschau is simple as it is easily accessible from major cities such as Cologne and Düsseldorf. The quickest way to reach this gem of a town is by driving, which would take roughly an hour and a half. Alternatively, you could also take a train to Aachen and then hop on a bus to Monschau. The journey may take longer than driving but offers a great opportunity to appreciate the picturesque scenery along the way.

Upon entering this quaint town, you will be immediately captivated by its fairy tale-like atmosphere, characterized by vibrant window-box flowers adorning the medieval-style buildings. A must-visit location is the Monschau Castle (Burg Monschau), perched high above the town center. Once the abode of German nobility, today, it serves as a youth hostel with regular guided tours available for visitors wishing to learn more about this historical monument. The panoramic views from the castle terrace overlooking the village and Rur valley are simply spectacular.

Another popular site worth visiting is the Red House (Rotes Haus), home to a prosperous cloth merchant family in the 18th century. It now serves as a museum that offers glimpses into well-preserved rooms that showcase beautiful Rococo and Empire-style furniture along with silverware, porcelain artifacts, and art collections.

Meandering through the narrow streets of Monschau, you'll discover enchanting shops selling traditional German crafts such as intricately carved wooden cuckoo clocks or fine lacework. An important stop on your journey should be the Monschau Glass Craft Center (Glashütte Monschau). Here, you'll find delicate, hand-blown glassware ranging from glass sculptures to tableware. You can even try your hand at glassblowing under the watchful eye of skilled craftsmen—an engaging hands-on experience not to be missed.

A trip to this charming town wouldn't be complete without indulging in some regional culinary delights. Local restaurants offer traditional German dishes, with many sourcing fresh ingredients from nearby farms. The famous Monschau mustard (Monschauer Senf) is a gourmet staple you must try served in a variety of flavors at the historic Senfmühle mustard mill.

For nature enthusiasts, the wild and romantic Eifel National Park surrounds Monschau and provides a fantastic opportunity for hiking and wildlife watching. The Vennbahn, one of Europe's longest railbike routes, passes through the area giving cycling enthusiasts an excellent way to explore the region.

Monschau retains its charm by staying untouched by modern advances while still offering modern conveniences to its visitors. Hosting a range of captivating events throughout the year such as traditional Christmas Markets or open-air stage productions in summer provides ample entertainment opportunities for visitors of all ages.

In conclusion, whether you're seeking to immerse yourself in history, picturesque landscapes, or gastronomic delights, Monschau is sure to capture your heart. This beautiful German town has something for everyone and promises a delightful travel experience unlike any other. Why wait? Pack your bags and embark on a memorable journey to enchanting Monschau.

Hallstatt, Austria

Nestled between the towering Dachstein Mountains and the glimmering waters of Lake Hallstatt lies the idyllic village of Hallstatt, Austria. This picturesque destination offers a unique blend of natural beauty, cultural attractions, and rich history that leaves visitors enchanted and yearning for more.

Upon arriving in Hallstatt, one's vision is instantly captured by the quaint pastel-colored houses lined along the lakefront, creating a postcard-esque setting unrivaled by many. The village is known for its magnificent baroque architecture, showcasing the region's intricate craftsmanship and attention to detail.

The appeal of Hallstatt goes beyond its visual charm, as the village offers an array of activities and attractions tailored to satisfy every traveler's wish list. Whether you desire relaxation or adventure, this quaint Austrian village caters to all preferences.

For history buffs and curious minds alike, a visit to the Hallstatt Salt Mines is an unforgettable experience. Believed to be the oldest salt mine in the world, this unique attraction takes visitors on an intriguing journey through time. Don a traditional miner's outfit before descending into the depths of the mine to explore its ancient passageways. Alongside impressive subterranean salt lakes and chambers carved by prehistoric miners awaits a thrilling ride on Europe's longest wooden slide—a memory you won't soon forget!

Nature lovers will revel in opportunities to immerse themselves in the awe-inspiring vistas that surround Hallstatt. Lace-up your hiking boots for an invigorating trek up Mount Dachstein via various trails, or traverse the Five Fingers viewing platform for panoramic views of the Austrian Alps that will take your breath away. For those seeking a more leisurely stroll, walk along Lake Hallstatt's perimeter while soaking up its tranquility and beauty.

Another must-visit site awaits at the entrance to Echern Valley: Hallstatt's unique ossuary, known as the Beinhaus. This small, 12th-century chapel houses the skulls and bones of over 1,200 former inhabitants, providing a glimpse into local customs regarding the deceased. Adorned with flowery wreaths and intricate carvings, the skulls' unique decoration reflects a deep respect for ancestry and tradition.

No visit to Hallstatt is complete without a boat ride on Lake Hallstatt. Rent a traditional wooden rowing boat, or take a scenic tour aboard an electric vessel. The tranquil waters provide prime opportunities for photography, so have your camera ready to capture snapshots of fairy-tale charm around every bend.

Hungry from a day of exploration? Indulge in Austrian cuisine at one of Hallstatt's many lakeside eateries. Savor dishes like Schnitzel, Käsespätzle (cheese noodles), and freshly-caught fish while enjoying unobstructed views of the picturesque landscape.

As evening descends upon this enchanting haven, the village comes alive with a warm glow illuminating the waterfront promenade—perfect for an intimate stroll after dinner. Unwind in one of Hallstatt's cozy accommodations, ranging from family-owned guesthouses to luxurious hotels, creating an ideal home away from home.

Hallstatt's beguiling beauty makes it an unforgettable destination for travelers seeking to uncover Austria's hidden gems. Its charming streets, fascinating history, and mesmerizing scenery will leave you spellbound—we invite you to venture off the beaten path and discover the magic that awaits in Hallstatt.

Dinant, Belgium

Belgium, a small European nation known for its medieval towns and Renaissance architecture, is rich in history and culture. One of its many hidden gems is Dinant, a picturesque city located along the Meuse River. With its stunning natural surroundings and numerous historical sites, Dinant is definitely worth adding to your travel itinerary.

Situated between towering cliffs and the sparkling Meuse River, Dinant's breathtaking landscape will captivate you from the moment you arrive. Its most iconic symbol is the Collegiate Church of Notre Dame de Dinant, a 13th-century Gothic cathedral featuring a distinct onion-shaped bell tower. This impressive landmark can be seen from various points around the city and serves as a constant reminder of Belgium's architectural heritage.

One of the main reasons travelers visit Dinant is to explore its rich history. Known as the birthplace of Adolphe Sax, the inventor of the saxophone, the city celebrates his legacy with an eponymous museum. At Maison De Monsieur Sax, you'll discover not only Sax's life story but also exhibits tracing the instrument's development over time. If you time your visit right, you might even be able to attend the International Adolphe Sax Competition or one of many lively jazz festivals throughout the year.

Another historical site worth visiting is the Citadel of Dinant. Perched high above the city on a rocky outcrop, this fortress has played a crucial role in several wars since its construction in 1040. A cable car will whisk you up to explore its halls and enjoy panoramic views over the city and river below. Don't miss out on seeing the haunting First World War trenches as well as learning about Dinant's military past through guided tours or interactive exhibits at the on-site museum.

Dinant's geological treasures aren't limited to its picturesque setting; it also boasts a fascinating network of caves waiting to be explored. Grotte La Merveilleuse, discovered in 1904, is a must-visit for sightseers and adrenaline junkies alike. Step into its depths to be astonished by its array of stalactites and stalagmites as you learn about this otherworldly environment. For a more physically demanding experience, consider kayaking or canoeing down the Lesse River – a tributary of the Meuse – as it winds through picturesque valleys and past ancient castles.

If you're a fan of Belgium's world-famous brews, then Dinant has something special in store for you. The Leffe Brewery, located near the city, is open to visitors who want to learn about the art and history of beer-making or sample its various flavors during a guided tour. Be sure to pay a visit to Le Creuset, an atmospheric cafe tucked into a cave near the Collegiate Church. Here, you can enjoy local beers while soaking up Dinant's unique ambiance.

Dinant is a captivating destination that effortlessly combines history, adventure, and relaxation. With its architectural marvels, rich cultural heritage, and stunning natural attractions, it provides visitors with a genuine taste of Belgian charm. Wander along its quaint cobbled streets and let yourself be immersed in this idyllic city's beauty - and perhaps even be inspired to return again someday.

Troyes, France

Located in the heart of the Champagne region, Troyes is a picturesque medieval French town that offers a unique blend of history, culture, and elegance. With its half-timbered buildings, cobblestone streets, and enchanting atmosphere, Troyes is undoubtedly one of France's hidden gems that should not be missed by travel enthusiasts.

As you arrive in Troyes, you will immediately be captivated by its intriguing architecture and historical significance. The narrow alleys and winding streets create an intimate setting where visitors can immerse themselves in the rich heritage and stories of this charming town. From its ancient churches to exquisite museums and art galleries, here are some of the must-visit attractions to include in your itinerary when traveling to Troyes.

The Saint Peter and Saint Paul's Cathedral is an impressive gothic structure that stands tall amidst the town's skyline. With its giant rosette windows and soaring vaulted ceilings, one can't help but admire the intricate details that unveil the artistic mastery behind this grand edifice. The cathedral also houses a superb collection of Aubusson tapestries depicting scenes from the life of Jesus.

One of Troyes' most iconic landmarks is the Church of Saint Jean au Marché. With its stunning stained-glass windows and distinctive wooden statues, this church is the perfect testament to Troyes' past flourishing in artistry and craftsmanship during medieval times. Sitting in the same square as the church is the market where Joan of Arc persuaded King Charles VII to continue his journey to Reims for his coronation during the Hundred Years' War.

A visit to Troyes would be incomplete without experiencing its magnificent museums showcasing centuries-old artifacts. The Museum of Fine Arts and Archaeology (Musée des Beaux-Arts et d'Archéologie) presents a fascinating collection that ranges from Roman remains to French impressionist paintings. Similarly, the Museum of Modern Art (Musée d'art moderne) houses an extensive array of contemporary artworks by renowned artists such as Gauguin, Matisse, and Renoir.

While strolling through the town, visitors can also marvel at the beautifully preserved half-timbered houses that are typical of medieval architecture in Troyes. These unique structures feature a striking blend of both dark wooden beams and warm earth-toned colors. For an authentic taste of medieval architecture, pay a visit to La Maison de l'Outil et de la Pensée Ouvrière (The House of Tools and Workers' Thought), which showcases a stunning array of antique tools while unraveling the history of handcrafted traditions.

As the birthplace of France's iconic champagne industry, Troyes is perfectly situated for wine enthusiasts to explore the many lush vineyards and cellars scattered across the countryside. Embark on a guided tour to learn about the intricate process involved in crafting the world's most celebrated sparkling wine while sampling a variety of champagne flavors.

Finally, indulge in Troyes' delectable culinary offerings at one of its many mouth-watering restaurants or bistros. Savor traditional dishes like andouillette, a type of sausage made from pork intestines—known exclusively as Andouillette de Troyes—or sample some of Troyes' regional specialties such as Chaource cheese and praline macarons.

With its captivating history, architectural splendor, and intoxicating charm, Troyes promises a memorable voyage through time that echoes with every footstep along its cobblestone streets. So venture off the beaten path and embrace this alluring destination that truly embodies all the magic that France has to offer.

Ronda, Spain

Discover the Beauty of Ronda, Spain: A Breathtaking Destination for Travel Enthusiasts

Nestled among the picturesque cliffs of Spain's Andalusian region, Ronda is a city steeped in history and charm. This magical destination captivates travelers with its stunning landscapes, ancient architecture, and rich cultural heritage. In this article, we'll explore what makes Ronda an unforgettable vacation spot and offer some tips for planning your next trip to this beautiful corner of Spain.

Ronda's rich history dates back thousands of years, with evidence of human habitation as early as the Neolithic era. The city was later inhabited by the Celts, Romans, Visigoths, and Moors before being conquered by the Catholic Monarchs in 1485. This diverse past has left its mark on Ronda's distinctive architecture and cultural traditions.

One of the city's most iconic landmarks is the Puente Nuevo (New Bridge), which spans the spectacular 120-meter-deep Tajo gorge. Completed in 1793 after more than 40 years of construction, this breathtaking feat of engineering connects Ronda's old Moorish town with its more modern districts. Visitors can immerse themselves in the city's past by exploring its labyrinthine streets and marveling at historic buildings like Palacio de Mondragon and the Church of Santa Maria la Mayor.

A trip to Ronda offers an authentic taste of Andalusian culture. The city is famous for its vibrant festivals, such as Feria Goyesca – a colorful celebration that pays tribute to legendary Spanish painter Francisco Goya. Held each September, this event features a week-long program of bullfighting tournaments, flamenco performances, and traditional parades complete with elaborate costumes.

Another must-see attraction in Ronda is Plaza de Toros, one of the oldest bullrings in Spain. While the practice of bullfighting remains controversial, the carefully preserved arena provides fascinating insights into this classic Spanish tradition and the region's proud equestrian history.

Exploring Ronda's culinary scene is a pleasure for food lovers. The city boasts a diverse range of dining options, from cozy tapas bars to upscale restaurants serving modern Andalusian cuisine. Local specialties include rabo de toro (bull's tail), an oxtail stew cooked in a rich tomato and red wine sauce, and Serrano ham, thinly sliced from aged hams produced in nearby villages.

Don't leave Ronda without sampling its famous wines. The region is renowned for its winemaking, with vineyards producing high-quality reds and whites to accompany your meal or take home as a souvenir.

Ronda's natural beauty offers endless opportunities for outdoor enthusiasts. Hike along rugged cliffside trails in El Tajo Gorge, taking in panoramic views of the surrounding countryside. Or, for more experienced climbers, tackle the challenging route up La Hoya del Tajo – a steep limestone massif that towers above the city.

If watersports are more your style, the nearby Guadiaro River provides an idyllic setting for kayaking and rafting adventures. In addition, horseback riding through Ronda's picturesque hinterland is the perfect way to experience its beautiful landscapes up close.

Easily reachable from Costa del Sol or Malaga via car or train, Ronda offers a unique and unforgettable vacation experience. With its rich history, vibrant culture, delectable food and wine, and endless opportunities for adventure in stunning natural surroundings, it's a destination that should be on everyone's bucket list.

Bruges, Belgium

Nestled in the heart of Europe, Bruges is a true gem that often goes under the radar. This fairy-tale town in Belgium takes visitors on a journey through time, thanks to its picturesque cobblestone streets and stunning medieval architecture. Known as the "Venice of the North," Bruges is packed with romantic canals, historic churches, and inviting market squares that make it a must-visit destination for travelers exploring Europe.

The heart of Bruges lies in its medieval charm. The well-preserved buildings and narrow alleyways transport visitors to the past when wealthy merchants filled their pockets by trading on these very streets. Today, you can still find an array of delightful artisan shops and cozy cafés dotted along these lanes, offering everything from home-made chocolates to mouth-watering waffles.

One major draw for visitors to Bruges is its historic city center, a UNESCO World Heritage site. The Markt square is surrounded by imposing medieval buildings such as the Belfry Tower and the Cloth Hall. The Belfry Tower has been an emblematic symbol of Bruges for centuries. 366 steps lead to the top of this 83-meter high monument, which offers a breathtaking panoramic view over the city.

Another must-visit site in Bruges is the Church of Our Lady, boasting the tallest tower among brick-built structures in Belgium. The church houses one of Michelangelo's most famous sculptures, Madonna and Child. Additionally, art lovers will be delighted by Groeningemuseum; a prestigious museum displaying an impressive collection of works from renowned artists such as Jan Van Eyck, Hans Memling, and Hieronymus Bosch.

A boat tour through the intricate network of canals is also a quintessential experience while visiting this mesmerizing city. As you glide past elegant mansions and under quaint stone bridges, you'll discover hidden gardens and picturesque waterfronts that will leave you in awe. A canal tour is a fantastic way to explore Bruges' most memorable sites, including its charming chapels and majestic palaces.

Gastronomy in Bruges is as diverse and delightful as its architecture. The city is known for its rich tapestry of mouth-watering cuisines—from traditional Flemish dishes such as 'moules frites' and Belgian waffles to international culinary delights. And let's not forget the famed Belgian chocolate! Renowned for its exceptional taste, you won't be able to resist the temptation of indulging in this national treasure.

In addition to its gastronomic appeal, Bruges has earned a reputation as a prominent beer destination. Sample some of Belgium's best brews at local haunts such as 2be Beer Wall or the historical De Halve Maan Brewery. They offer interesting tours that incorporate the history of brewing in Bruges with an opportunity to taste some refreshing local beers.

Bruges truly comes alive during the holidays with a festive Christmas market taking over its central cobblestone squares. Colorful, wooden stalls offer everything from unique crafts and holiday treats to mulled wine and wintery delights that no visitor should miss.

In conclusion, Bruges is a city where history unsurprisingly converges with modernity to create an unforgettable fusion of charm, culture, and cuisine. From admiring its architectural marvels to indulging in decadent chocolate, visitors to Belgium should ensure that exploring the enchanting streets of Bruges is high on their list of things to do during their journey through Europe.

Lincoln, England

Nestled in the heart of the English countryside, Lincoln is a historic city that offers a unique blend of ancient history, modern amenities, and stunning landscapes. Whether you're a history enthusiast or simply looking for a relaxing getaway, Lincoln has something for everyone. This article highlights some of the best attractions and experiences you can enjoy while visiting this charming city.

A trip to Lincoln wouldn't be complete without exploring its rich history, starting with Lincoln Cathedral. This awe-inspiring structure dominates the city's skyline and is one of the finest examples of Gothic architecture in Europe. The cathedral's intricate craftsmanship and fascinating stories are sure to leave you captivated. Be sure to join one of the guided tours to learn more about this remarkable building's history.

Just a stone's throw away from the cathedral is Lincoln Castle. This historic fortress was built by William the Conqueror in 1068 and is home to one of only four surviving copies of the Magna Carta. You can wander through its impressive ramparts and delve into its ancient dungeons, discovering centuries-old artefacts along the way. Don't miss your chance to take part in a guided tour led by costumed characters who will transport you back in time with their engaging storytelling.

For history enthusiasts looking for even more excitement, visit the nearby Museum of Lincolnshire Life, which offers an immersive insight into local life between 1750 and 1940. The collection features everything from Victorian workshops to vintage tractors and provides an interactive experience for visitors young and old.

After exploring these historical sites, take some time to stroll down Steep Hill. This picturesque street is lined with independent shops, boutiques and cafes, making it perfect for a leisurely afternoon browse or coffee break. The charming winding lanes that surround Steep Hill are also well worth exploring – you'll find hidden gems like jewellers, art galleries and cosy pubs around every corner.

If you're an art lover, The Collection Museum should not be missed. This modern space houses a vast selection of contemporary and historical art, including fine art works by JMW Turner and John Piper. The museum also features regularly changing exhibitions, ensuring there's always something fresh to see.

In addition to its rich history and culture, Lincoln is surrounded by stunning natural beauty. Take a leisurely walk along the Fossdyke Canal Trail, which runs for six miles alongside the city's Roman waterway. Alternatively, if you're feeling more adventurous, venture out to Hartsholme Country Park where you can explore 200 acres of picturesque woodlands, lakes and parkland.

For food enthusiasts, there's no shortage of delicious dining options in Lincoln. The city is home to a diverse range of restaurants serving up international cuisines and traditional English fare. Whether you're craving classic fish and chips or searching for sophisticated fine dining experience, you're sure to find it here.

Of course, no trip to England would be complete without sampling some local ales at a traditional British pub. Lincoln has a variety of historic inns where you can enjoy a pint or two while learning about the fascinating past of these ancient establishments.

In conclusion, Lincoln is truly a hidden gem in the English countryside that offers an abundance of history, culture and natural beauty. From its breathtaking cathedral and castle to its charming streets and thriving arts scene, there are countless reasons why this city should be at the top of your travel bucket list. Pack your bags and embark on your next adventure – Lincoln awaits!

Delft, Netherlands

Nestled amidst the picturesque province of South Holland, Delft is a charming city that exudes timeless beauty. Known for its rich history, mesmerizing canals, and the famous Dutch artist Johannes Vermeer, this must-see destination has something in store for every traveler. Let us delve into the wonders of Delft and explore the various elements that make it a dream destination.

The historic city center of Delft tells tales as colorful as its iconic ceramics. The Markt Square is an excellent starting point to get acquainted with the city's splendors. It is surrounded by impressive edifices like the Nieuwe Kerk (New Church) – the final resting place of several members of the Dutch Royal Family – and Stadhuis (City Hall), with its stunning Renaissance architecture.

One cannot visit Delft without marveling at its centuries-old churches. Oude Kerk (Old Church), with its mesmerizing stained glass windows and leaning tower, is a sight to behold. Paintings by various accomplished artists adorn both Old and New churches, while their towers provide breathtaking panoramic views of the city.

Delft is known for its renowned blue pottery, a legacy spanning over 400 years. The Royal Delft Museum showcases exceptional examples of this unique craft, and visitors can even try their hand at painting their own ceramic masterpiece.

Art enthusiasts must not miss a visit to Het Prinsenhof (the Prince's Court), where they can immerse themselves in Dutch history through exhibits that include manuscripts, ancient tombs, and relics from William of Orange's life. A special section in the museum is dedicated to Johannes Vermeer, showcasing his artistry and impact on Dutch art.

The canals weaving through Delft's city center are a vital part of its charm. A leisurely stroll or a picturesque boat tour is the perfect way to soak in the city's stunning canal houses, historic bridges, and vibrant street life. Some of the must-see canals include Oude Delft, Wijnhaven, and Nieuwe Delft.

Delft has harnessed wind energy for centuries with its enchanting windmills. Molen de Roos (the Rose Windmill) offers an intriguing insight into Dutch lifestyle, culture, and industry. Visitors can explore the inner workings of the mill and witness how wheat is ground into flour. The observation deck atop provides fantastic views of Delft's skyline.

Immerse yourself in nature at Delftse Hout, Delft's local recreation area where you can rent a bike or canoe to explore lush greenery and serene water bodies. Do not miss the annual Koningsdag (King's Day) celebrations – a lively event that marks the monarch's birthday with joyous festivities, fun fairs, and colorful markets.

After a day full of exploration, relishing local cuisine is inevitable. Delft boasts a plethora of cafes, restaurants, and bakeries that cater to diverse taste buds. Delight in traditional delights like poffertjes (mini pancakes), stroopwafels (caramel-filled waffles), or kibbeling (deep-fried fish).

Delft captivates visitors with its rich cultural heritage, stunning architecture, and natural beauty. From ambling along its captivating canals to following in the footsteps of Vermeer or enjoying authentic Dutch cuisine, there is always something to cherish in this quaint Dutch city.

Central Europe

Cesky Krumlov, Czech Republic

Cesky Krumlov is a charming town located in the southern part of the Czech Republic. With its well-preserved medieval architecture and picturesque surroundings, it is a popular destination for travelers from all over the world. It is a UNESCO World Heritage site that beckons to travelers seeking a taste of Europe's rich history and culture. Amidst winding cobblestone streets and beautifully preserved architecture, Cesky Krumlov offers an unforgettable experience that will leave you longing for more.

As you step into this captivating town, the first thing you'll notice is its stunning centerpiece: the imposing Cesky Krumlov Castle. This magnificent structure, dating back to the 13th century, bears witness to the history and power that once resided here. Today, visitors can marvel at its grandeur on one of its guided tours or simply appreciate its beauty from afar.

The castle not only boasts striking architecture but also features lush, meticulously maintained gardens. Within these gardens are various installations, including a revolving auditorium where open-air performances take place throughout the summer months. The panoramic views from these gardens are simply breathtaking – providing a vista that encompasses both the charming town below and the Vltava River embracing it.

Explore further into Cesky Krumlov by wandering through its quaint streets and alleys. As you stroll through town, you'll feel as if you've been transported back in time. The historic houses, some over 500 years old, are adorned with intricate frescoes showcasing distinct art styles and motifs from various periods in history. These beautifully maintained facades lend an air of romance to Cesky Krumlov's narrow streets.

While exploring this enchanting town, be sure to pay a visit to St. Vitus Church. This Gothic-style cathedral towers high above Cesky Krumlov and demands attention with its compelling design. The church's ornate interior is adorned with stunning religious artwork, captivating all who enter its hallowed halls. Attending a musical performance within its walls is a truly magical experience, with the church's acoustics bringing each note to life.

One cannot visit Cesky Krumlov without indulging in traditional Czech cuisine. Throughout the town, you'll find numerous eateries offering local delights such as hearty goulash, svickova, and smoked meats. Be sure to sample some trdelnik, a sweet pastry rolled in sugar and cinnamon, often filled with ice cream or whipped cream - it's the perfect treat as you explore this charming town.

No journey to Cesky Krumlov would be complete without experiencing its vibrant culture firsthand. Throughout the year, the town plays host to various festivals and events. Each June, visitors are transported back to medieval times during the Five-Petalled Rose Festival - a weekend-long event showcasing live music, traditional crafts, and theatrical performances.

As evening falls over Cesky Krumlov, be swept away by the town's enchanting nightlife. The Old Town Square comes alive with outdoor cafes and cozy restaurants offering al fresco dining beneath twinkling strings of lights. For those seeking entertainment, live music can be found in hidden courtyards or at one of the many historic taverns that dot Cesky Krumlov's streets.

With its fairy tale-like charm, rich history and culture, and picturesque scenery, Cesky Krumlov is an unforgettable destination that will surely captivate any traveler's heart. So pack your bags and allow yourself to be transported back in time as you embrace the magic of this Czech Republic treasure.

Pécs, Hungary

Nestled in the rolling hills of Southern Hungary, lies the charming city of Pécs. Rich in history, culture and natural beauty, this hidden gem offers a truly unique travel experience. Home to a fascinating blend of Roman, Turkish and medieval architecture, art lovers and history enthusiasts alike will find plenty to discover in the enchanting streets of Pécs.

Getting to Pécs is a breeze with various transportation options available. Travelers can fly into Budapest or

Osijek (Croatia), followed by a scenic train or bus ride that showcases the region's picturesque countryside. Alternatively, for those who prefer a more leisurely journey, renting a car and taking the Southern Transdanubian highway allows for freedom to explore on one's own terms.

Upon arrival, visitors are greeted by the majestic Pécs Cathedral, an iconic structure dominating the city's skyline. Constructed during the 11th century, this Romanesque marvel has been expanded and renovated numerous times throughout history - a testament to how interwoven faith is with Pécs' identity.

Next to the cathedral lies Szechenyi Square, a vibrant plaza bustling with life and energy. This busy hub is surrounded by eclectic eateries serving delectable local delicacies such as sztrapacska and catfish paprikash. Enjoy alfresco dining while marveling at the city's pastel-colored baroque facades, or visit one of its cozy 'pince' wine bars that offer delightful Hungarian wines.

For art aficionados, Pécs is paradise. The Zsolnay Cultural Quarter houses studios of artists whose ceramic masterpieces dazzle visitors with their intricate designs. One must not miss the Museum of Fine Arts showcasing exclusive local paintings alongside works by renowned international artists such as Rembrandt and Monet.

Those enamoured by ancient history must visit Cella Septichora, an archaeological site boasting an impressive collection of 4th-century Christian monuments. This

UNESCO World Heritage site is a labyrinth of tombs, crypts and chapels that illustrates the life and beliefs of the early Christian community.

A short stroll away lies the Pécs Synagogue, a monumental testament to Hungary's rich Jewish legacy. Restored after being heavily damaged during World War II, its grandeur still echoes the once-prominent Jewish community's contributions to Pécs' vibrant history.

For some downtime amidst nature, venture out to the Mecsek Mountains. These lush green hills offer various hiking trails, leading to breathtaking vantage points that flaunt panoramic views of the city. The picturesque Mecsek landscape is perfect for relaxing or indulging in activities like horse riding and mountain biking.

Finally, surreal beauty awaits at the Lake Orfu resort area - an ideal locale to enjoy water sports or take a leisurely canoe ride through pristine scenery. Surrounded by rolling hills, dense forests and quaint Hungarian villages, this tranquil setting offers reprieve from bustling city life.

As evening falls upon Pécs, its thriving nightlife beckons party-goers with trendy pubs and clubs dotting Kiraly Street. From contemporary dance halls to underground hangouts seeped in history, there's something for everyone seeking a entertaining night out on the town.

In conclusion, Pécs is a true revelation for travelers seeking a culturally stimulating yet off-the-beaten-path European adventure. With its fascinating history spanning multiple eras, awe-inspiring architecture and warm-hearted people, a visit to Pécs promises an unforgettable escapade into old-world charm tinged with modern delights.

Bratislava, Slovakia

As the capital of Slovakia, Bratislava may not be as well-known as its popular European counterparts like Paris, Rome, or Barcelona, but it is a hidden gem that should never be underestimated. With its rich history, unique architecture, and vibrant cultural scene, Bratislava offers an authentic and unforgettable travel experience.

Nestled along the Danube River, the historic city of Bratislava is a perfect destination for those seeking a mix of old-world charm and modern sophistication. From its imposing castle perched atop a hill to its quaint cobblestone streets lined with charming cafés, there is no shortage of picturesque spots to explore.

Getting to Bratislava has never been easier with several transportation options available. Whether you choose to arrive by plane via the M.R. Štefánik Airport or decide to take a scenic train ride from neighboring cities such as Vienna or Budapest, you'll find yourself immersed in Slovakian culture in no time.

Bratislava's Old Town is perhaps the city's most popular area for visitors, and for good reason. Here you can enjoy several iconic landmarks, including Michael's Gate, the medieval entrance to the city; St. Martin's Cathedral, an impressive Gothic church that once crowned Hungarian kings; and Primate's Palace, an 18th-century architectural wonder showcasing exquisite frescoes and tapestries.

Another unmissable attraction in Bratislava is its majestic Castle. A symbol of power since the 9th century, this impressive fortress has been continuously rebuilt over the centuries and now serves as a museum housing a fascinating collection of artifacts spanning various historical eras.

For those seeking respite from history and culture buffs' usual spots like museums or landmarks, head just outside Old Town to SNP Square. This bustling hub hosts various events throughout the year, including the famed Bratislava Christmas Market. The market offers the opportunity to indulge in traditional Slovakian dishes such as kapustnica (cabbage soup), trdelník (sweet pastry), and mulled wine while browsing artisanal crafts and trinkets.

Evening entertainment is abundant in Bratislava. You can catch a show at the renowned Slovak National Theatre or dive into the local music scene at one of the city's many live music bars. Of course, a trip to Bratislava isn't complete without sipping on some fine Slovakian beer at a traditional pub like Klastor or Slovak Pub.

If you're up for exploring a bit further, there are plenty of local destinations nearby that you can easily visit for a quick day trip. Visit the magical Bojnice Castle or take in the captivating beauty of Slovak Paradise National Park, both just a couple of hours away by car or public transportation.

Lastly, don't forget to bring home some tokens of your travels! Typical souvenirs from Bratislava include ceramics, embroidered textiles, and honey wine, locally known as medovina. These unique gifts are sure to delight friends and family – or serve as mementos of your unforgettable journey.

Bratislava is a hidden treasure that offers an exceptional travel experience for those who venture off the beaten path. With its rich history, stunning architecture, delectable cuisine, and welcoming atmosphere, this captivating city deserves its place in your European itinerary.

Bled, Slovenia

Bled, a picturesque town in the heart of Slovenia, is often overshadowed by its more renowned neighbors. However, this hidden gem boasts natural beauty and a rich cultural heritage that makes it the perfect destination for any travel enthusiast. From exploring mesmerizing landscapes to immersing yourself in local traditions, there are countless reasons why a journey to Bled should be on every traveler's bucket list.

Nestled amidst the Julian Alps, Bled's breathtaking scenery will captivate you from the moment you arrive. The sparkling turquoise waters of Lake Bled encompass a small island where the ancient Church of the Assumption proudly stands – an iconic symbol of the town's history and traditions. A gentle stroll around the lake offers awe-inspiring views of this captivating scenery, accentuated by deep emerald forests and towering snow-capped mountains that surround this idyllic locale.

For those seeking adventure, Bled provides ample opportunities for outdoor enthusiasts to indulge in their favorite activities. Hiking trails around the lake and up into the surrounding hills reward travelers with panoramic vistas of unspoiled nature. Meanwhile, watersport lovers can revel in kayaking or paddle boarding on Lake Bled's placid waters. A short distance away, adrenaline junkies can find exhilarating activities like paragliding and canyoneering within the pristine Triglav National Park.

No trip to Bled would be complete without a visit to Bled Castle, perched majestically atop a hill overlooking the lake. This medieval fortress transports visitors back in time as they explore its intriguing museum and fascinating history. The castle also offers exquisite dining experiences accompanied by stunning views – perfect for those special moments or simply unwinding after a day filled with adventure.

Bled is not only known for its picturesque landscapes but also its delicious cuisine. One must-try delicacy while visiting is the traditional Bled Cream Cake – "kremšnita." This exquisite layered pastry filled with fluffy cream and topped with a delicate dusting of powdered sugar is guaranteed to delight your taste buds. Local restaurants also offer a broad selection of dishes inspired by its diverse and rich culinary history. From hearty goulash to fresh trout caught in the very lake you admire, the flavors of Bled cater to any food lover's desires.

To truly immerse yourself in the local culture, consider timing your visit to coincide with one of Bled's annual festivities. The Bled Days Festival, typically held in July, celebrates the town's heritage through live music performances, street food from local vendors, and an enchanting fireworks display that lights up the night sky. On another note, the International Music Festival showcases classical talent from around the globe, allowing visitors to enjoy world-renowned artists while exploring this delightful destination.

Despite being a small town, Bled offers a wide range of accommodations to suit any traveler's needs. Cozy bed and breakfasts overlooking the lake provide an intimate setting for romance or relaxation, while modern hotels within walking distance cater to families and groups seeking comfort and convenience. Regardless of your choice in lodging, you'll find yourself immersed in welcoming hospitality befitting this charming Slovenian town.

Bled's alluring beauty is matched only by its incredible ambiance. With its enchanting landscapes, thrilling outdoor activities, tantalizing cuisine, and vibrant cultural experiences – this hidden gem of Slovenia promises an unforgettable adventure that will leave you longing for a return trip. So pack your bags and prepare to be bewitched as you journey into the heart of Bled.

Wroclaw, Poland

Situated on the banks of the Oder River, Wroclaw is a vibrant city in western Poland that offers travelers a unique mix of history, culture, and picturesque scenery. This enchanting city, once known as Breslau and now referred to as the "Venice of Poland," has been shaped by a rich and complex past. With its charming architecture, numerous bridges, and lively atmosphere, Wroclaw is a must-visit destination for those seeking an authentic and unforgettable Polish experience.

History enthusiasts will be delighted by Wroclaw's stunning array of architectural gems that narrate its storied past. The city's Old Town has been artfully restored after suffering heavy damage during World War II, allowing visitors an opportunity to step back in time as they stroll through this picturesque area. Here, travelers will encounter the Market Square, an expansive plaza adorned with colorful baroque buildings showcasing eye-catching facades. Dominating the square is the elegant Gothic-style Wroclaw Town Hall – an iconic structure featuring intricate stonework and a remarkable astronomical clock.

A visit to Wroclaw would be incomplete without exploring its most famous attraction - Ostrow Tumski or Cathedral Island. This serene location is steeped in history and spirituality, with its foundation dating back to the 10th century. Impressive churches such as St. John the Baptist Cathedral grace this island, where visitors can admire stunning religious relics and ornate interior designs. For those seeking a tranquil retreat from the lively city center, this atmospheric enclave is an ideal destination to indulge in some peaceful contemplation.

Wroclaw is often dubbed "The City of Bridges" due to its over 100 bridges connecting various parts of the city across picturesque waterways. Taking a leisurely stroll along these canals or embarking on a boat tour along the Oder River offers outstanding views of Wroclaw's skyline and riverside landscapes. Be sure not to miss the legendary "Lovers Bridge," a popular spot for couples to fasten padlocks as a symbol of their lasting love.

Art aficionados will relish Wroclaw's thriving cultural scene, which includes numerous art galleries, studios, and museums displaying works that span different mediums and genres. The National Museum houses an extensive collection of art that includes Silesian and Polish masterpieces - the perfect destination for those seeking to immerse themselves in the region's artistic heritage.

No trip to Wroclaw is complete without embarking on a search for its famous bronze dwarves. These sculptures are scattered throughout the city, commemorating Pro-democracy movement The Orange Alternative's playful protests against the oppressive Communist regime in the

1980s. With over 350 miniatures to be found throughout Wroclaw, tourists can join organized dwarf-hunting tours or engage in their own whimsical explorations.

After a day spent exploring the city's many attractions, visitors can indulge in Wroclaw's exquisite culinary scene. From traditional Polish eateries serving up dishes such as pierogi (dumplings) and bigos (hunter's stew) to sophisticated fine dining establishments presenting global cuisine, there is something to satisfy every palate.

Wroclaw is a captivating city that boasts a rich tapestry of historical architecture, picturesque landscapes, and contemporary culture. This alluring destination promises an unforgettable experience for travelers who venture off the beaten path to experience its many charms. So if you're planning your next European getaway, consider a visit to the unforgettable city of Wroclaw, Poland.

Eger, Hungary

Eger, a picturesque city in the northern region of Hungary, is a hidden gem just waiting to be explored by adventurous travelers. From its rich history and captivating architecture to its delectable cuisine and vibrant wine culture, Eger offers visitors a travel experience unlike any other.

Your journey should begin with a visit to the iconic Castle of Eger, perched atop a hill overlooking the city. This remarkable fortress' history dates back to the 13th century and played a crucial role in defending Hungary against Ottoman invasions. Roaming through its ancient walls, towers, and underground passages is both an educational and thrilling experience for all ages. Be sure to visit the Gothic Palace and Heroes' Hall for an immersive look into the past of this incredible fortress.

A short walk from the Castle of Eger, you'll find Dobo Square, the heart of the city where locals and tourists alike gather to revel in its bustling atmosphere. Surrounded by stunning Baroque architecture, Dobo Square houses several prominent attractions such as the Minorite Church and István Dobó Statue. The square often hosts various cultural events and festivals throughout the year that showcase Hungarian art, music, and gastronomy.

Don't miss out on visiting one of Hungary's largest churches - Eger's Basilica, built between 1831-1836 in neoclassical style. The awe-inspiring dome measures at 54 meters high and is adorned with magnificent frescoes portraying scenes from biblical stories. Be sure to attend one of their enchanting organ concerts or enjoy some quiet moments amidst the calming echoes within this sacred space.

Eager to unwind after a day of exploration? Eger has you covered with its famous thermal baths, offering a relaxing respite for weary travelers. The city's most popular choice is Eger's Turkish Bath, which was originally established during the Ottoman rule in the 17th century. Soak in these rejuvenating waters and embrace the centuries-old tradition of bathing culture in Hungary.

Embark on a sensory journey through traditional Hungarian flavors at numerous local restaurants and eateries within Eger. Savor dishes like goulash (a rich beef stew), chimney cake (a sweet spiral-shaped pastry), or lángos (fried dough topped with sour cream and cheese). Be sure to enjoy your meal with a glass of Egri Bikavér, the city's signature red wine also known as "Bull's Blood."

Conclude your adventure in Eger with a visit to the Valley of the Beautiful Women, a quaint area famous for its numerous wine cellars. Enjoy guided wine tastings and savor different varietals while learning about the rich traditions and history of winemaking in this region. The valley also offers numerous outdoor seating areas that provide stunning views, perfect for sipping your newfound favorite wines as you reminisce about your unforgettable journey through Eger.

Eger, Hungary offers an incredible experience steeped in history, beauty, culture, and mouth-watering cuisine that will leave you yearning for more. Embrace your adventurous spirit and explore this enchanting city tucked away amidst picturesque hills and vineyards. Before long, you'll find yourself captivated by its charm, treasure trove of stories, and warm-hearted residents who are eager to share their love for their captivating city with all who visit.

Sandomierz, Poland

Sandomierz, an enchanting town in southeastern Poland, offers travelers a unique and memorable experience. Steeped in rich history and natural beauty, it is a hidden gem that captivates the hearts of visitors from around the world.

Founded over 1,000 years ago, Sandomierz is a historical treasure with a picturesque old town that takes you back in time. The stunning architecture of St. Michael's Cathedral and the Old Town Market Square will leave you astonished. The cathedral, built between the 14th and 17th centuries, serves as the heart of Sandomierz's religious history. In contrast, the Old Town Market Square offers quaint cafés and charming souvenir shops perfect for leisurely afternoons.

The Royal Castle is another must-visit site in Sandomierz. Dating back to the 14th century, this magnificent castle once served as a royal residence during Poland's golden age. Its imposing gothic façade and majestic towers add to its grandeur. Inside, visitors are treated to an exquisite collection of paintings and historical artifacts that recount Poland's fascinating past.

Sandomierz is also famed for its Opatowska Gate and underground city. The Opatowska Gate is a remnant of medieval defensive walls that protected the city centuries ago. This impressive structure provides an incredible panoramic view from its tower. The underground city – a network of over 30 interconnected cellars - allows visitors to delve into Sandomierz's rich history even further by giving them a unique glimpse into medieval trade and life.

Nature lovers are not left out as Sandomierz boasts several beautiful parks and gardens perfect for spending tranquil moments or taking scenic strolls. For water enthusiasts, the serene Vistula River is ideal for canoeing or rafting. But one of the most breathtaking attractions in Sandomierz is the Peacock Garden, a stunning park surrounding a palace with an intriguing history. Complete with peafowls roaming freely, exploring the garden will leave you enchanted at every turn.

When it comes to culinary delights, Sandomierz has an array of mouth-watering traditional Polish dishes waiting to be savored. Try Pierogi, tasty dumplings filled with ingredients such as cheese, meat or mushrooms – a foodie's delight! For dessert, treat yourself to the famous Sandomierz gingerbread, which has delighted sweet-toothed visitors since the 16th century.

Getting to Sandomierz is relatively easy, with several transport options available. You can choose to fly into nearby airports like Rzeszow-Jasionka or Lublin and then take a bus or train ride to reach the town. Alternatively, a self-drive trip from Warsaw or Krakow is an excellent option for those wanting to explore Poland's countryside.

Accommodation options in Sandomierz are varied to cater to any taste or budget. You can find cozy guesthouses that exude local charm, modern hotels that help you stay connected while on the go, or even Airbnb rentals for a more authentic experience.

Traveling to Sandomierz is a journey into Poland's captivating past and picturesque present. With its wealth of historical attractions, natural beauty, and mouth-watering cuisine, this charming town guarantees an unforgettable experience for all who venture there. Add Sandomierz to your travel bucket list and let this hidden gem of Poland enthrall you with its timeless charm and allure.

Ljubljana, Slovenia

Located in the heart of Europe, Ljubljana, the vibrant and picturesque capital city of Slovenia, awaits your visit. This enchanting city, whose name means "beloved" in Slovenian, is the perfect travel destination for anyone seeking a perfect blend of history, culture, and urban charm. With its rich architectural legacy and multitude of attractions, Ljubljana will capture your heart and leave an indelible impression on your memory.

Ljubljana has a unique appeal that combines elements of both Eastern and Western Europe with its own distinct Slovenian flair. Set under the watchful gaze of the medieval Ljubljana Castle perched on a hilltop, the city's well-preserved Old Town entices visitors with its picturesque lanes and vibrant outdoor cafes. From the iconic Triple Bridge to the bustling Central Market,

Ljubljana offers an array of experiences that cater to every traveler's whims.

Begin your journey by soaking in the city's architecture as you wander through its charming streets. The Old Town is filled with Baroque-style buildings such as the Robba Fountain and St. Nicholas Cathedral. However, one must not miss out on witnessing Ljubljana's Art Nouveau gems – simply stroll along Miklošičeva Street or visit cultural centers like Križanke and Dragon Bridge.

One cannot leave without indulging in Ljubljana's thriving culinary scene that is a treat for every food lover. Enjoy traditional dishes such as žlikrofi (Slovenian dumplings) or kranjska klobasa (Carniolan sausage) at a local tavern or try some fusion cuisine – this small yet diverse city offers flavors from around the world. Dine alfresco in a riverside cafe while sipping on local wines as you watch street performers in the bustling Prešeren Square.

Nature lovers will appreciate the city's green spaces and the fact that it was awarded the European Green Capital title in 2016. Take a leisurely stroll through the beautiful Tivoli Park, or rent a bicycle and explore the city's extensive network of bike lanes, weaving through the lush landscape that surrounds Ljubljana. Just a short drive away, you can embark on an adventure in Slovenia's great outdoors: hike through forest trails, visit breathtaking waterfalls, or set sail across pristine Alpine lakes.

Ljubljana also boasts a thriving creative scene filled with art galleries, museums, and vibrant street art. Engage your cultural side at the National Museum of Slovenia or drop by Metelkova – an alternative culture hub where artists, activists, and free spirits alike gather to celebrate creativity.

The charm of Ljubljana extends beyond its attractions to its warm-hearted people who are always ready to welcome you with open arms. The city's intimate atmosphere guarantees that even first-time visitors feel like returning friends rather than strangers.

Empty your bucket list as you immerse yourself in this magnificent city with endless opportunities for exploration and enjoyment. Whether you're admiring ancient architecture, sampling world-class cuisine, embracing nature's beauty or participating in cultural events – Ljubljana provides it all.

So pack your bags and prepare to be charmed by Ljubljana's unforgettable blend of history, culture, and scenic beauty – a destination that truly exemplifies what it means to be "beloved."

Mediterranean Europe

Zadar, Croatia

Travelers from across the globe flock to the enchanting coastal city of Zadar, Croatia. Rich in history, breathtaking landscapes, and a unique blend of old and new, Zadar guarantees an unforgettable experience for anyone seeking a European adventure.

Overlooking the crystal-clear waters of the Adriatic Sea, Zadar has a rich and diverse history dating back more than 3,000 years. It was once home to ancient Roman, Byzantine, and Venetian settlements, giving the city a remarkable charm with its historic sites. Visitors can explore numerous archaeological treasures, including the Roman Forum built by Emperor Augustus around 1 BC and the Church of St. Donatus built in the 9th century.

As you wander through Zadar's cobbled streets and historic squares, be prepared to be captivated by its unique atmosphere. The seamless blend of old-world charm and contemporary facilities creates an extraordinary setting for visitors to immerse themselves in Croatian culture fully.

One of the most iconic attractions in Zadar is its famous Sea Organ - an experimental musical instrument built into marble steps along the waterfront. Designed by architect

Nikola Bašić in 2005, it uses natural airflow and tidal movements to create soothing melodies that echo throughout the city's coastline. So grab a seat on one of these marble steps as you gaze out at the shimmering waters of the Adriatic and listen to this magical symphony composed by nature itself.

Another artistic masterpiece by Bašić includes Greeting to the Sun - where photo-voltaic cells create intriguing patterns of vibrant colors as evening falls. The installation pays tribute to Zadar's world-renowned sunsets that are best admired from Café Bar Fosa or Arsenal Bar, which provide panoramic views over the archipelago reserved for National Parks – Kornati Islands.

The culinary experience in Zadar adds to its allure. From traditional peka (veal or seafood cooked under a bell-shaped dome) to the local cheeses of Pag Island, the diverse flavors of authentic Croatian cuisine will leave you craving more. And you won't want to miss sampling the sweet Maraschino liqueur made from the famous Dalmatian Maraska cherry.

For those seeking outdoor activities, Zadar offers a range of options that cater to all interests and fitness levels. You can take a leisurely bike ride along scenic coastal routes, hike through Paklenica National Park, or visit awe-inspiring waterfalls of Krka National Park – where you can even swim in its crystal-clear pools. Alternatively, embark on an island-hopping tour; explore the Kornati Islands' rugged beauty, sail around Ugljan and Pasman islands or discover charming fishing villages on nearby Pag and Dugi Otok islands.

For an enriching cultural experience, attend one of Zadar's numerous festivals occurring throughout the year. The Zadar Outdoor Festival showcases adventurous sports, while Zadar Summer Festival presents top-class music, theatre, and art performances from local and international artists.

When you combine modern city amenities with ancient history, stunning natural wonders, delicious food and exceptional cultural experiences, it is no wonder why Zadar ranks among each traveler's dream destination list. The magical appeal of this sun-drenched Croatian gem makes it a must-visit for anyone seeking a remarkable journey brimming with unforgettable moments. So pack your bags and set out for the captivating city of Zadar - your next great adventure awaits!

Kotor, Montenegro

Kotor, a picturesque coastal town nestled at the foot of Lovćen Mountain in Montenegro, promises an unforgettable experience for anyone seeking adventure and beauty. With its rich history, pristine beaches, and breathtaking landscapes, Kotor offers the perfect blend of relaxation and excitement for both intrepid travelers and laid-back vacationers.

A UNESCO World Heritage Site, Kotor's Old Town is a marvel of medieval architecture. Here, ancient cobblestone streets wind between the centuries-old buildings adorned with intricate frescoes, transporting visitors back in time. Begin your journey by exploring the narrow alleys and hidden squares to soak in the history and charm of this enchanting town.

The iconic Kampana Tower stands tall as a testament to Kotor's fortifications throughout the ages. For those looking for an invigorating challenge, climb the 1,350 steps to St. John's Fortress (San Giovanni Castle), which offers panoramic vistas of the Bay of Kotor and beyond. Be sure to carry a bottle of water and a camera as you traverse these historic ramparts.

If maritime heritage is your passion, make sure to visit the Maritime Museum in Kotor. This well-curated museum showcases artifacts showcasing Montenegro's tradition of seafaring families and their contributions to maritime history. The artifacts include old navigation maps, ship models, antique navigational instruments, and marine paintings.

Beyond the confines of Old Town awaits an abundance of outdoor adventures for nature enthusiasts. Take a boat tour or rent a kayak along the beautiful Bay of Kotor – sometimes referred to as Europe's southernmost fjord – where hidden caves and secluded beaches await discovery.

A visit to Our Lady of the Rocks Church on a man-made island is another must-do on your trip to Kotor. Accessible only by boat from nearby Perast town, this charming church is decorated with delicate frescoes and houses a fascinating museum full of historical artifacts and exquisite paintings.

For those who thrive on adrenaline, paragliding is available just 30 minutes away from Kotor in Budva. Float effortlessly above the town, relishing stunning aerial views of Sveti Stefan Island, Budva's beaches, and the azure Adriatic.

Of course, no trip to Montenegro would be complete without savoring the delicious local cuisine. Wander through the bustling markets and find an authentic "konoba" (tavern) to indulge in a variety of culinary delights such as "ngoče" (black mussels), "burek" (flaky pastries filled with cheese, meat, or sweet fillings), and local cheeses paired with a glass of Montenegrin wine.

Lastly, no journey to Kotor is truly complete without reveling in the vibrant nightlife. As dusk turns to night, prepare for a memorable time exploring unique bars tucked within Old Town's streets and alleys or dance at the trendy clubs lining the marina.

Whether you're seeking adventure, relaxation or an immersive cultural experience, Kotor is an enchanting destination that will leave lasting memories. From its ancient architecture and compelling history to its breathtaking landscapes and mouthwatering cuisine, there's something for everyone to fall in love with during a visit to Kotor, Montenegro. So pack your bags and embark on this unforgettable journey!

Valletta, Malta

Situated on the picturesque Mediterranean coastline, Valletta, the charming capital city of Malta, is a captivating blend of rich history, stunning architecture, and buzzing atmosphere. Whether you're a history buff, an art enthusiast or just looking for a memorable escape, Valletta has something for every traveler.

As you wander through the narrow cobblestone streets of this UNESCO World Heritage site, you'll be enticed by the stunning Baroque architecture that adorns the cityscape. One such architectural gem is St. John's Co-Cathedral - a masterpiece commissioned in the 16th century by the Knights of St. John. As you step inside this awe-inspiring site, you'll be greeted by opulent interiors adorned with intricate carvings and mesmerizing frescoes created by the famed Italian painter Caravaggio.

Another must-visit attraction in Valletta is the Grand Master's Palace. This historic building has served as the residence of Maltese leaders for centuries and now houses the president's office and the Maltese Parliament. As you explore its lavish rooms, don't forget to check out the Palace Armoury - a treasure trove containing an impressive collection of suits of armors and weapons from different periods.

To delve deeper into Maltese history, head to Fort St Elmo on the tip of Valletta's peninsula. This star-shaped fortress played a crucial role in defending Malta against invaders and offers breathtaking views of Marsamxett Harbour and Grand Harbour.

After exploring Valletta's historical sites, take a stroll through the vibrant Upper Barrakka Gardens. These beautifully landscaped gardens offer panoramic views across Grand Harbour and are home to several statues and monuments that celebrate Malta's rich past. As you relax beneath palm trees and exotic plants, watch out for one of Valletta's most beloved traditions - the daily firing of the Saluting Battery at noon.

Don't forget to indulge in Malta's delicious cuisine during your time in Valletta. The city boasts an array of phenomenal restaurants catering to every palate. To experience authentic Maltese flavors, be sure to try rabbit stew, pastizzi (a flaky pastry filled with ricotta or peas), and ftira (a traditional Maltese bread). For those with a sweet tooth, devour the famed Maltese dessert imqaret - a delectable concoction of dates encased within golden, deep-fried dough.

Valletta is also a hub for the arts and offers an exciting range of events and festivals throughout the year. The Malta International Arts Festival is a must-attend event for art enthusiasts, while music lovers should definitely check out the annual Valletta International Baroque Festival or the exciting Notte Bianca - a night-long celebration of culture and creativity.

Getting around Valletta is a breeze thanks to its compact size. Its pedestrian-friendly streets make walking an ideal mode of transport, though buses and taxis are also easily available for those looking for a quick ride.

A trip to Malta would not be complete without exploring its glistening turquoise waters. Take advantage of Valletta's coastal location by opting for a harbor cruise or embarking on a tour to nearby islands such as Comino or Gozo.

Valletta is an enchanting city filled with beauty, history, and culture that truly caters to every kind of traveler. Its unique allure makes it one destination you simply cannot afford to miss on your next European adventure.

Lucca, Italy

Lucca, a picturesque city located in the heart of Tuscany, Italy, is an enchanting destination for travelers seeking a unique and unforgettable experience. With its rich history, stunning architecture, and exceptional cuisine, a journey to Lucca promises to captivate and inspire all who visit.

As you approach Lucca, you are immediately struck by the historic city walls that surround and protect the city. These impressive walls date back to the Renaissance era and provide an excellent starting point for exploration. Take a leisurely stroll or bike ride atop the 4-kilometer long path on the walls while admiring breathtaking views of the cityscape and surrounding countryside.

Stepping into Lucca's historic center transports you back in time with its well-preserved medieval buildings, narrow cobblestone streets, and enchanting piazzas. Be sure to visit Piazza dell'Anfiteatro, a charming square built on the site of an ancient Roman amphitheater. The distinctive elliptical shape of the piazza invites visitors to explore its array of cafes, shops, and restaurants while absorbing its captivating atmosphere.

Lucca boasts several stunning churches that shouldn't be missed during your visit. The Cathedral of St. Martin is a remarkable example of Romanesque architecture featuring intricate artworks and sculptures, including the incomparable masterpiece "The Incoronation of the Virgin" by Tuscan artist Jacopo della Quercia. Likewise, San Michele in Foro is another splendid church adorned with remarkable details that leave visitors marveling at its beauty.

Another must-see attraction in Lucca is Torre Guinigi, a 44-meter high tower crowned with a rooftop garden where holm oaks grow majestically. Climbing 230 steps may be an arduous task, but once you reach the top of the tower, you are rewarded with panoramic views of Lucca's terracotta rooftops and the magnificent Tuscan hills in the distance.

No journey to Lucca is complete without indulging in the mouthwatering cuisine that represents the region's culinary heritage. Sample traditional Lucchese dishes such as tortelli lucchese, a delicious pasta stuffed with seasoned meat or vegetables and topped with a rich meat sauce. Be sure to pair your meal with a local wine from nearby vineyards, like Montecarlo or Colline Lucchesi.

Lucca also offers visitors the opportunity to partake in various cultural events throughout the year. In October, the annual Lucca Comics & Games festival attracts comic book enthusiasts and gamers from around the world, transforming the city into a playground for fans of pop culture. Additionally, summer months bring an array of concerts as part of Lucca Summer Festival, featuring international artists performing at open-air venues.

For those wishing to further explore Tuscany, Lucca serves as an excellent base from which to discover other gems in the region. The breathtaking cities of Florence and Pisa are easily reachable by train or car for day trips, while the idyllic landscapes of Chianti and Val d'Orcia beckon travelers seeking adventure and relaxation amidst verdant rolling hills and picturesque vineyards.

Lucca offers a truly remarkable experience that combines history, culture, culinary delights, and breathtaking natural beauty. Plan your visit to this captivating Italian city, where you will discover memories that will last a lifetime.

Matera, Italy

Traveling to Matera, Italy is an unforgettable experience that immerses one in rich history, stunning landscapes, and a unique culture. Nestled in the rugged terrain of the Basilicata region in southern Italy, Matera is known for its ancient cave dwellings, called sassi, which date back over 7,000 years. This UNESCO World Heritage Site is not only an extraordinary testament to human ingenuity but also a living breathing city that offers a once-in-a-lifetime opportunity to explore and embrace the enduring spirit of Italy.

The journey to Matera begins with a sense of anticipation as one takes in the picturesque vistas along the way. The landscape is a harmonious blend of rolling hills, rocky outcrops, and verdant valleys that provide a breathtaking backdrop to the town perched atop. Upon arrival, one can't help but feel awestruck by the beauty and charm of this timeless destination.

A visit to Matera's famous sassi districts, Sasso Caveoso and Sasso Barisano, transports travelers back in time as they wander through meandering streets flanked by ancient dwellings. These cave homes were originally built by early inhabitants seeking refuge from invading forces and harsh weather conditions. Over centuries, these simple abodes evolved into more complex structures adorned with intricate frescoes and architectural details.

As one explores the labyrinthine pathways of these earth-hugging dwellings, it's impossible not to feel a sense of reverence for those who have called this magical place home throughout history. The intertwining warren of caves provides snapshots into different eras: from prehistoric settlements to Byzantine frescoed chapels, each corner reveals layers of Matera's storied past.

One must-see attraction during a trip to Matera is the city's collection of rupestrian churches. These sanctuaries carved into soft tufa rock are adorned with frescoes created by Byzantine monks. Among these ancient chapels is the 13th-century Crypt of Original Sin, often referred to as the "Sistine Chapel of Rupestrian Art," which boasts colorful frescoes depicting Old Testament scenes and early Christian symbolism.

Aside from its historical sites, Matera brims with vibrant arts, culture, and cuisine. The town hosts a plethora of festivals throughout the year, celebrating everything from jazz and film to traditional Lucanian culture and cuisine. Signature culinary delights include crusty breads, hearty pastas, flavorful cheeses, and a variety of locally produced wines that will entice any food enthusiast. Authentic Italian dining at Osteria al Casale or sampling delectable pastries at Pasticceria Royale offers a truly indulgent experience.

In addition to its rich history and cultural traditions, Matera also provides ample opportunities for ecotourism and outdoor adventure. The surrounding region is perfect for long treks through pristine nature reserves such as the Parco della Murgia Materana. This park, which spans across a plateau dotted with ravines and caves, boasts not only diverse flora and fauna but also impressive prehistoric rock art.

Accommodation in Matera ranges from elegant boutique hotels like Sextantio Le Grotte Della Civita to quaint bed-and-breakfast establishments carved into the very rock itself. These unique lodgings allow visitors to fully immerse themselves in the town's remarkable atmosphere while simultaneously offering luxurious comforts.

In a world where modernity has rapidly overtaken tradition, Matera stands as a beautiful testament to human adaptability and resilience. Its haunting beauty endures despite centuries of hardship, earning it rightful recognition as the 2019 European Capital of Culture. For travelers seeking an awe-inspiring journey filled with ancient marvels, picturesque beauty, cultural immersion, delightful gastronomy, and warm hospitality, Matera is an absolute must-visit destination.

Hvar, Croatia

Hvar, a picturesque island off the coast of Croatia, has long been a sought-after destination for travelers seeking both relaxation and adventure. With its stunning natural beauty, rich history, and vibrant culture, Hvar offers a unique and memorable experience for anyone who wishes to explore its captivating charms.

One of the most striking features of Hvar is its breathtaking scenery. The island is characterized by lush rolling hills, where vineyards and olive groves thrive under the warm Mediterranean sun. The coastline boasts an array of enchanting bays and beaches, each offering visitors a chance to soak up the sun and enjoy the crystal-clear waters.

The town of Hvar, often referred to as the Queen of the Dalmatian Islands, is situated on the island's southern coast. This beautiful town serves as an excellent base for exploring the island's many attractions. The cobblestone streets and historic buildings reflect Hvar's rich heritage, while the numerous cafes, bars, and restaurants provide a lively atmosphere for both locals and tourists.

A must-see site in Hvar town is the ancient hilltop fortress known as Fortica Španjola. Its strategic position offers panoramic views of the town below and the surrounding islands. Besides its military significance in past centuries, Fortica Španjola now serves as a museum showcasing artifacts from Hvar's rich history.

Hvar also offers several opportunities for outdoor enthusiasts to connect with nature. Adventurous spirits can hike through fields of lavender - for which Hvar is famous - that stretch across the western part of the island. Another popular hiking destination is Sveta Nikola, the highest peak on the island standing at 628 meters above sea level. Those who brave this climb are rewarded with spectacular views of Hvar and its neighboring islands.

If water-based activities are more appealing, visitors can take advantage of Hvar's crystal-clear waters by participating in various water sports such as kayaking, sailing, and snorkeling. Boat tours are also available to explore the stunning Pakleni Islands – a group of small islets off the coast of Hvar. These islands are home to secluded beaches and coves which can only be accessed by boat, providing an idyllic setting for a relaxing day trip.

The island's vibrant cultural scene further enhances any visit to Hvar. Annual music, art, and food festivals showcase local talent and give visitors an insight into the island's traditions and customs. The Hvar Summer Festival is arguably the most popular event, taking place from June to September and featuring concerts, theater performances, and other cultural events in various historic venues throughout the town.

Those who wish to indulge in local delicacies will not be disappointed by Hvar's gastronomic delights. Traditional Croatian cuisine emphasizes fresh seafood, locally-grown vegetables, and high-quality olive oil. Visitors can sample various tasty dishes such as "gregada," a fish stew with onions, potatoes, and white wine or "peka," a slow-cooked meat dish often made with lamb or veal.

Hvar's bustling nightlife caters to a wide variety of tastes. From beachside bars with live music and charming wine cellars to energetic nightclubs boasting international DJs, there is something for every type of partygoer.

Hvar promises a uniquely captivating experience for all. Its natural beauty combined with its rich history, culture, and enticing outdoor adventures ensure that visitors to this enchanting Croatian island will create unforgettable memories that last a lifetime.

Eastern Europe

Sofia, Bulgaria

Sofia, the bustling capital of Bulgaria, is an alluring city that seamlessly blends centuries of history with modern urban charm. Positioned at the foothills of Vitosha Mountain, Sofia entices travelers with its diverse architecture, rich history, and vibrant culture. Traveling to this fascinating city offers you an opportunity to explore a host of landmarks and attractions.

One of Sofia's main landmarks is the Alexander Nevsky Cathedral, a majestic neo-Byzantine edifice that dominates the skyline. Completed in 1912, this architectural marvel was built in honor of the Russian soldiers who lost their lives fighting for Bulgaria's independence during the Russo-Turkish War (1877-1878). The cathedral's gilded domes and intricate mosaics make it a must-visit spot for any traveler interested in history or architecture.

Vitosha Mountain serves as both a natural backdrop and an outdoor playground for Sofia residents and visitors alike. Accessible via public transportation or by car, Vitosha offers a range of recreational activities, including hiking, skiing, snowboarding, and mountain biking. The mountain also contains several picturesque monasteries worth visiting, such as the medieval Dragalevtsi Monastery.

Returning to the city center, you'll find another historical gem: Boyana Church. A UNESCO World Heritage site, this medieval Bulgarian Orthodox church features stunning 13th-century frescoes that are considered among the most significant examples of Eastern European medieval art. It's advised to book your visit in advance as admittance is limited to preserve this precious artistic treasure.

The National Palace of Culture (NDK) is another noteworthy attraction in Sofia. This imposing building houses various event spaces dedicated to theater performances, concerts, exhibitions, and conferences. Its striking Brutalist architecture makes it impossible to miss when wandering through Sofia's streets. If you happen to visit in December or January, the NDK square becomes a lively Christmas market, complete with festive stalls, an ice-skating rink, and the perfect atmosphere for holiday cheer.

For a taste of Sofia's vibrant culinary scene, head over to Vitosha Boulevard. Here, you'll find numerous restaurants and cafes showcasing the best of Bulgarian cuisine. Be sure to try local dishes like shopska salad (a mix of fresh tomatoes, cucumbers, peppers, onions, and cheese), banitsa (a savory pastry filled with cheese or spinach), and kebapcheta (grilled minced meat rolls).

Sofia's thriving arts community is best represented by its many galleries scattered throughout the city. Visit the National Gallery for Foreign Art (Natfiz) to peruse an eclectic mix of European art from various periods. Or stop by Sofia City Art Gallery for thought-provoking contemporary exhibitions.

Finally, no trip to Sofia would be complete without exploring its Roman roots. The Ancient Serdica Archaeological Complex offers a fascinating glimpse into the city's past through well-preserved Roman ruins. This historical site even includes an open-air museum displaying reconstructed walls, streets, and buildings from ancient Serdica.

Sofia is a captivating city that amazes its visitors with multifaceted beauty and history. Whether it's ancient ruins or mouth-watering cuisine that sparks your interest, Sofia offers something for everyone and promises an enchanting travel experience you won't soon forget.

Sighisoara, Romania

Nestled in the heart of Romania, the stunning medieval city of Sighisoara is a must-visit destination for travelers seeking a journey back in time. With its rich history, well-preserved architectural gems, and warm hospitality, this enchanting city offers an unforgettable experience for all who venture within its walls.

A trip to Sighisoara begins with an exploration of its most famous landmark: the iconic Clock Tower. Towering over the city at an impressive 64 meters tall, this 14th-century marvel serves as the main entrance to Sighisoara's walled old town. As you climb its narrow staircase and ascend towards the sky, be prepared to be captivated by mesmerizing panoramic views of the city below.

Beyond the Clock Tower lies a labyrinth of cobblestone streets and colorful baroque buildings that transport visitors to a bygone era. Among these historic structures is the charming Birthplace of Vlad Dracul – better known as the infamous Vlad III Dracula, who inspired Bram Stoker's fictional vampire count. Today, this centuries-old house has been transformed into a museum and restaurant where visitors can learn about Vlad's life and even sample some traditional Romanian dishes.

As you wander through Sighisoara's old town, be sure not to miss The Church on the Hill - one of the city's most important religious monuments. This stunning gothic church is worth the climb up nearly 200 covered wooden steps known locally as Scholar's Stairs, which were initially built in 1642 to help students reach a nearby school during harsh winters. Once at your destination, you'll be greeted by breathtaking frescoes and centuries-old tombstones adorning its walls.

For more insight into the area's history and local culture, stop by The History Museum of Sighisoara. Here, you'll find a treasure trove of artifacts that chronicle the city's story, from its 12th-century founding by Saxon craftsmen to its present-day status as a UNESCO World Heritage site. In addition, the museum hosts temporary exhibitions, enriching your understanding of this magical city further.

While exploring Sighisoara, make sure to drop by The Covered Staircase. It is a unique attraction that dates back to the 17th century and offers a remarkable view when you climb on top of it. This historical landmark is representative of the skilled craftsmanship found throughout the entire city.

After a day of touring Sighisoara's many attractions, you'll undoubtedly develop an appetite for traditional Romanian cuisine. You can find delicious local fare such as sarmale (cabbage rolls), mici (spicy minced meat rolls), and papanasi (doughnut-like pastries) at many of the city's cozy and welcoming restaurants. Pair these dishes with a glass of fruity Romanian wine for an authentic dining experience that perfectly encapsulates your journey in this extraordinary town.

But your adventure doesn't end with sunset. As the sun casts its final rays over the city's rooftops and night falls upon Sighisoara, embrace the stillness and beauty of this enchanting medieval gem further illuminated under soft streetlights' glow. And as you stroll along its quiet lanes or admire its shimmering landmarks from afar, know that your memories forged here will forever be ingrained within you.

Visiting Sighisoara, Romania, promises an unforgettable experience steeped in history, culture, and medieval charm. This well-preserved city is not just a living testament to Romania's past but an enchanting destination that every avid traveler should explore at least once in their lifetime.

Tallinn, Estonia

Tallinn, the capital city of Estonia, is a hidden gem waiting to be explored by avid travelers. With its rich history, stunning architecture, and vibrant culture, this Baltic destination offers a unique and unforgettable experience.

One of the highlights of traveling to Tallinn is exploring its Old Town, a UNESCO World Heritage site. This well-preserved medieval city center is filled with cobblestone streets, historic buildings, and charming squares. Stroll through the narrow alleyways, visit the iconic Alexander Nevsky Cathedral, and admire the panoramic views from Toompea Hill.

As you wander through the streets, you'll come across numerous cafes, restaurants, and shops. Taste traditional Estonian cuisine, indulge in local delicacies like black bread, smoked fish, and homemade pickles. Don't forget to try the famous Estonian drink, Vana Tallinn, a sweet rum-based liqueur.

In addition to its historical charm, Tallinn also boasts a vibrant and modern side. The city is known for its thriving tech industry, which has earned it the nickname "Estonian Silicon Valley." Visit the Telliskivi Creative City, a former industrial complex turned hipster district, where you can explore trendy boutiques, art galleries, and enjoy live music performances.

Nature enthusiasts will find plenty to explore in Tallinn as well. Take a short ferry ride to the nearby islands of Nõmmeveski and Prangli to enjoy pristine beaches, picturesque landscapes, and peaceful hiking trails. These islands offer a perfect retreat from the hustle and bustle of the city.

Tallinn also hosts various festivals and events throughout the year, such as the Tallinn Music Week and the Christmas Market. These events showcase the city's vibrant cultural scene, offering music, art, and delicious local treats.

When it comes to accommodation, Tallinn offers a range of options to suit every traveler's preferences. From luxury hotels to budget-friendly hostels and cozy guesthouses, there is something for everyone. Consider staying in the heart of the Old Town for a truly immersive experience.

Traveling to Tallinn is like stepping into a fairy tale. Its enchanting Old Town, modern attractions, and natural beauty make it a perfect destination for those seeking a unique and memorable trip. Whether you're interested in history, culture, or simply enjoying the lively atmosphere, Tallinn has it all. So pack your bags and get ready to embark on an unforgettable adventure in this charming Baltic city.

Riga, Latvia

Riga, the capital city of Latvia, invites modern-day adventurers to explore its vibrant culture, rich history, and architectural splendors. Set on the Baltic Sea's southern shores and nestling at the heart of the Baltic States, this enchanting city promises an unforgettable travel experience for all who visit.

The first step to any Riga adventure is a visit to its picturesque Old Town. This UNESCO World Heritage Site boasts a labyrinth of cobblestone alleys teeming with hidden treasures waiting to be discovered. Wander around Vecrīga, the historical center of Riga, and marvel at the medieval churches, ancient guild halls, and beautifully restored buildings that span many centuries.

One of Riga's most iconic architectural attractions is St. Peter's Church. With a history dating back to 1209, this Gothic masterpiece showcases unique structural elements and stunning artwork that encapsulates various styles from different periods. The collection includes wooden sculptures dedicated to Saint Christopher and Saint Maurice and several Baroque paintings. For a small fee, visitors can take a glass elevator to the top of its 72-meter high tower for phenomenal city views.

Riga's Dom Cathedral is another must-visit attraction for sightseers. Built in 1211 and renowned as one of Northern Europe's largest medieval churches, this awe-inspiring building houses a 6,768-pipe organ that has delighted audiences since the early 19th century.

Art lovers should make a point to visit the unmissable Art Nouveau district in central Riga. This area stands testament to architect Mikhail Eisenstein's genius – his ability to merge multiple European styles creates an eclectic mix that characterizes Riga's distinctive identity. Spend time admiring some of these architectural gems such as Alberta iela and Elizabetes iela that feature stunning facades adorned with mythological creatures, intricate floral motifs, and ornamental details.

Central Market, one of Europe's largest and oldest markets, delivers a unique sensory experience to travelers. Get a feel for the local culture as you navigate its five different pavilions dedicated to meat, fish, dairy products, vegetables, and gastronomy. Prepared to be tantalized by the mouth-watering aroma of traditional Latvian dishes such as Rupjmaize – a dark rye bread, Sklandrausis – a sweet and savory potato pie, or Pelēkie zirņi ar speķi – a hearty dish made from grey peas and bacon.

No visit to Riga is complete without soaking in the city's vibrant nightlife scene. From intimate jazz clubs like Trompete Taproom & Bar to lively bars such as Ala Folk Club that offers traditional Latvian beer and live music every night, Riga caters to all nighttime preferences. For those looking to catch live performances from local talents or well-rehearsed orchestras in an elegant atmosphere, Latvijas Nacionālais simfoniskais orķestris (Latvian National Symphony Orchestra) should be on your list.

Day trips are aplenty in Riga too – take advantage of the city's close proximity to beautiful natural areas like Gauja National Park or explore other nearby towns like Kuldīga and Jurmala for more cultural adventures.

The charms of Riga are abundant and captivating; its blend of old-world charm melded with contemporary influences make it an ideal destination for culture enthusiasts seeking new experiences. As you traverse this Baltic gem's streets, immerse yourself in its history, artistry, culinary delights, and lively atmosphere for an absolutely unforgettable journey that epitomizes true European grace.

Constanța, Romania

Constanța, the ancient city sitting on the picturesque coast of the Black Sea, is one of Romania's most underrated travel gems. As a thriving seaport with deep historical roots, there's so much to experience in this culturally rich city. From beach-filled summers to fascinating ruins and unique tastes of local cuisine, your trip to Constanța will be one to remember.

Begin your journey by exploring Old Town Constanța – an enticing fusion of old-world charm and modern vibrancy. Here, you'll find impressive examples of Roman and Byzantine architecture, richly painted Orthodox churches, and lively English-style tea houses. The central square, Piața Ovidiu houses stunning sculptures and ancient ruins lead you to uncover stories from the past whilst quaint boutiques and artistic ateliers offer exquisite finds.

No visit to Constanța is complete without unearthing its storied past at the History and Archaeology Museum. Showcasing captivating artifacts from various historical periods - including prehistoric times, Thracians, Greeks, Romans, Byzantines, and Ottomans - you'll gain a comprehensive understanding of the city's evolution.

Take a step back in time as you explore Tomis Harbor - an ancient port city filled with relics from Constanța's rich maritime history. Nestled by the waterfront lies the iconic Casino building; an Art Nouveau masterpiece that stands as a testament to Constanța's Golden Age during Romanian royalty.

The Roman Mosaic Edifice is another must-see historical site that displays intricate mosaic flooring remnants from the 4th century. This carefully preserved site beautifully illustrates the craftsmanship and elegance of Roman artistry in vibrant colors.

Discover miles of pristine beaches lining Romania's coastline as Constanța serves as the gateway to Mamaia resort - one of Eastern Europe's top summer destinations. Crystal-clear waters and golden sands stretch out invitingly, hosting visitors from all around the world. Here, you can unwind by the sea, indulge in thrilling water sports, or join a vibrant beach party as the sun sets.

Indulge your taste buds with the flavors of Constanța's local delicacies - heavily inspired by its history as a significant maritime hub. Seafood is an essential element, with dishes like fish stew and grilled fish being local favorites. You'll also find that Dobrujan cuisine, typical to the region of Dobrogea, exhibits Bulgarian and Turkish influences. Keep an eye out for unusual desserts such as sarailie - a syrup-soaked pastry with nuts and cream.

One of nature's finest spectacles - the Danube Delta - can be reached via Constanța, making for an unforgettable day trip. As Europe's second-largest river delta and a UNESCO World Heritage site, this labyrinth of waterways, floating reed islands, and diverse ecosystems create a haven for bird-watching enthusiasts seeking to spot rare species.

Finally, consider attending Constanța's annual festivals during your visit. From film festivals showcasing international talent to local celebrations honoring maritime culture or authentic folk traditions, these lively events are sure to leave lasting impressions.

A trip to Constanța, Romania is not just about visiting museums or enjoying sun-soaked beaches; it's an adventure into a rich narrative written through the ages. With its vibrant juncture at the edge of East and West - nature, history, culture, and cuisine converge seamlessly to offer unforgettable experiences along the shores of the Black Sea.

Saaremaa Island, Estonia

Estonia's largest island, Saaremaa, is a captivating destination that lures travelers with its natural beauty, historical landmarks, and peaceful atmosphere. This picturesque island boasts unspoiled landscapes and an alluring charm that provides an unforgettable experience to those visiting this hidden gem in the Baltic Sea.

With its scenic coastline, lush forests, and windswept fields of juniper bushes, Saaremaa is truly a paradise for nature lovers. One of the highlights of your visit should undoubtedly be Vilsandi National Park. Established in 1910 as the first nature reserve in Estonia, this park encompasses several smaller islands and enormous stretches of land filled with diverse flora and fauna. You can embark on guided hikes through the park or rent a bike to explore further afield – the choice is yours.

Saaremaa's rich history dates back to prehistoric times. The Kaali meteorite craters are one such fascinating spot that bears testament to this ancient past. Thought to have formed approximately 4,000 years ago as a result of multiple meteorites striking the area, these craters form an awe-inspiring geological feature worth seeing up close.

Another historically significant site on Saaremaa is the Kuressaare Episcopal Castle. Built in the 14th century during the Livonian Order's rule over Estonia, this well-preserved fortress remains an imposing sight today. It now houses the Saaremaa Museum – a must-visit destination during your stay on the island. This comprehensive museum tells the tale of Saaremaa and its people through various eras by showcasing archaeological finds, artworks, and interactive exhibits.

No trip to Saaremaa would be complete without experiencing one of its most famous exports – the traditional Estonian sauna. The authentic smoke saunas found across the island provide a rejuvenating experience that has been part of Estonian culture for centuries. Indulge yourself in hot steam, relax on the smooth wooden benches amid the scents of fragrant juniper branches, and finish with a refreshing dip in the cool sea.

During your stay, don't forget to sample the delicious local cuisine. Saaremaa's restaurants offer a variety of dishes made from locally sourced ingredients like fish, game, and berries. One regional specialty you must try is the hearty Saaremaa rye bread called "leib." This dense, dark bread is packed with flavor and makes a perfect accompaniment to any meal or enjoyed on its own as a tasty snack.

Getting to Saaremaa is an adventure in itself. The most common way to travel to the island is via a picturesque ferry ride from the mainland town of Virtsu. The hour-long journey offers stunning views over Estonia's western coastline and provides an exciting start to your trip.

Alternatively, adventurous travelers may choose to charter a yacht or sailboat to explore the island by sea.

While Saaremaa might be off the beaten path for most tourists visiting Estonia, this enchanting island offers a unique and unforgettable experience for those willing to venture beyond the mainland's well-trodden routes. From its pristine natural beauty and spellbinding historical sites to indulgent sauna experiences and delectable cuisine— you'll leave Saaremaa with memories that will last a lifetime.

Vilnius Lithuania

Nestled in the Baltic region of northeastern Europe lies Vilnius, the capital city of Lithuania. Known for its picturesque old town, diverse architecture, and rich cultural history, Vilnius has emerged as a top travel destination for those seeking off-the-beaten-path adventures. This article will guide you through the reasons why you should consider traveling to Vilnius and what to expect during your journey.

Vilnius is a vibrant city teeming with history dating back to its foundation in 1323. One of the most significant landmarks celebrating this historic legacy is Vilnius Cathedral, a stunning fusion of Neo-Classical and Gothic architectural styles constructed on the site where Lithuania embraced Christianity. The cathedral houses several important works of art, including frescoes by

Michelangelo Palloni and reconstructed interiors showcasing Lithuanian Baroque splendor.

Another must-see historical site in Vilnius is Gediminas Castle Tower. This iconic symbol of the city stands proudly above the Old Town on Castle Hill, providing stunning panoramic views of Vilnius's skyline. As you wander through the Old Town's cobbled streets and explore its medieval buildings like the Church of St. Anne, you'll quickly understand why UNESCO designated this area a World Heritage Site.

Vilnius's rich cultural tapestry reflects the city's diverse influences throughout its history. The Republic of Užupis, a self-proclaimed bohemian micronation situated within Vilnius's city limits, embodies this spirit with its quirky charm and artistic flair. Home to numerous art galleries, boutiques, and unique outdoor installations, Užupis is an ideal location for travelers seeking unconventional experiences.

Continuing with the theme of artistic expression, Vilnius hosts several well-known events that showcase local talent and creativity. One such event is the International Vilnius Film Festival, held each spring and considered one of the most prestigious events in Eastern Europe. Similarly, the Vilnius Jazz Festival attracts top international jazz musicians and aficionados for a week of electrifying performances each autumn.

Culinary enthusiasts will feel right at home in Vilnius, as traditional Lithuanian cuisine meets unexpected global influences. Local favorites like hearty "cepelinai" (potato dumplings filled with meat), "šaltibarščiai" (cold beet soup), and "kibinai" (meat-filled pastries) share the table with contemporary gastronomy at innovative restaurants. Vilnius's thriving café culture supports trendy coffee shops featuring specialty coffees and mouthwatering desserts for those seeking a more leisurely dining experience.

Nature lovers won't be disappointed when visiting Lithuania's capital. Green spaces abound throughout Vilnius, like Bernardine Gardens, which offer lush foliage, fountains, and sculptures alongside the tranquil Vilnia River. For a different perspective on the city's natural beauty, consider taking a hot air balloon ride above it all—all while marveling at the breathtaking aerial views.

Another option for outdoor enthusiasts is to explore Lithuania's countryside around Vilnius. With easy day trips to destinations like Trakai Island Castle or Europos Parkas (a vast open-air sculpture park), your itinerary can quickly fill with diverse sights and experiences that extend beyond the city limits.

Vilnius has much to offer travelers interested in experiencing its rich history, vibrant culture, mouth-watering cuisine, and beautiful landscapes. From historic Old Town streets and bohemian Užupis to world-class festivals and delectable dining options—there's no doubt that Vilnius should be on every intrepid traveler's bucket list.

Byala, Bulgaria

Nestled along the picturesque coastline of the Black Sea, Byala is a quaint Bulgarian town that has managed to escape the hustle and bustle of mass tourism. With its pristine beaches, charming local culture, and a treasure trove of history, Byala is an ideal destination for those who crave an authentic and peaceful travel experience.

As you venture into this charming town, you will be greeted with warm smiles and friendly faces that reflect the welcoming nature of the Bulgarian people. The town center consists of quaint shops, restaurants and cafes where you can savor delicious local cuisine while enjoying vibrant and lively conversations with locals.

One of Byala's most striking features is its stunning coastline. The beautiful sandy beaches stretch for miles and are dotted with small coves, providing ample opportunities for relaxation and privacy. In addition to being a sun-soaked haven for beach lovers, Byala offers abundant watersports activities such as sailing, windsurfing, and fishing. The clear blue waters provide excellent visibility for scuba diving and snorkeling enthusiasts who long to explore the rich marine life in these tranquil seas.

While lazing under the sun is undoubtedly appealing, Byala boasts numerous outdoor activities sure to capture your adventurous spirit. A favorite among visitors is exploring the lush countryside on foot or bike. Well-maintained trails meander through verdant hills offering breathtaking panoramic views of both land and sea. Along these paths you'll come across various vineyards which produce some of Bulgaria's finest wines – a visit here offers you a chance to discover another hidden gem within this picturesque town.

History buffs will revel in exploring the Stara Planina Mountains that surround Byala. The mountains house ancient architectural treasures like impressive monasteries which offer a glimpse into Bulgaria's past. Additionally, if you prefer discovering historical sites closer to town - venture into Old Town Byala where you'll find archaeological sites of ancient Greek and Roman settlements.

The region's Mediterranean climate provides the perfect excuse to indulge in the flavors of Bulgarian cuisine characterized by an eclectic mix of savory, sweet, and tangy. Byala is known for its fresh seafood dishes such as midye tava (fried mussels) and kalamar tava (fried squid), often paired with refreshing salads featuring local vegetables like tomatoes, cucumber, and peppers. Don't forget to try a glass of rakia, the traditional Bulgarian spirit or a glass of locally-produced wine.

Getting to Byala has never been easier, as it is located approximately 55 kilometers south of Varna and 75 kilometers north of Burgas. Both cities have international airports and are well connected by public transport to various destinations across Bulgaria, making it easy for travelers to access this stunning coastal town.

Accommodation options in Byala range from luxurious beachside hotels to smaller guesthouses that cater to different budgets. The town provides a comfortable stay without breaking the bank. While some of these accommodations offer views of the pristine shoreline others provide tranquil settings amid lush greenery for a serene escape.

Byala is undoubtedly a destination that offers an unforgettable experience for those who seek an authentic taste of Bulgaria without the stress of crowded tourist hotspots. So go off the beaten track and treat yourself to an enchanting vacation in this hidden gem along Bulgaria's beautiful Black Sea coast.

Sibiu, Romania

Sibiu, a picturesque city in the heart of Romania, should be at the top of any travel enthusiast's bucket list. With its rich history, enchanting architecture, and vibrant culture, Sibiu offers an unforgettable experience for those seeking adventure and discovery. This 500-word article will guide you through some of the must-see attractions and experiences that make Sibiu a unique destination.

Steeped in history, Sibiu was initially founded in the 12th century by Saxon settlers and has since evolved into a bustling metropolis. Nestled in the Transylvanian plateau, this charming Romanian gem is an essential stop for travelers who wish to immerse themselves in European culture.

As you amble through the cobblestone streets of Sibiu, one can't help but feel captivated by the city's medieval fortifications and pastel-colored Baroque buildings. The Council Tower, dating back to the 14th century and standing at thirteen stories high, delivers a panoramic view of Sibiu's Old Town that is a must-see for any visitor. Snap a quick photo before heading to the nearby Brukenthal National Museum or marvel at the astounding frescoes of Holy Trinity Orthodox Cathedral.

The Large Square (Piata Mare) is not only the center of Sibiu's historic quarter but also a hub of social activity throughout the year. During summer months, enjoy outdoor concerts and food festivals as you weave through lively throngs. In winter celebrations come alive with the annual Christmas market—regarded as one Romania's best—where visitors can indulge in steaming cups of mulled wine and pick up handcrafted holiday gifts.

A most curious attribute that stands out during your exploration of Sibiu would be some buildings' "eyes," which are small rooftop windows that make them appear as if they are observing passersby. These charming architectural features only add to the mystique of Sibiu and have become an iconic symbol of the city.

If you wish to take a break from strolling through the stunning streets, visit the beautiful Altemberger House— an exquisite example of Gothic architecture that now houses the Museum of History. Breathtaking exhibits include medieval weaponry, traditional pottery, and a variety of other historical artifacts.

For an authentic local experience, stroll Huet Square towards Liar's Bridge, a landmark surrounded by fascinating folklore and superstitious customs. The iron bridge is believed to creak when lies are spoken by those who cross it. Put this myth to the test and immerse yourself in local legend.

Sibiu's sublime countryside offers an excellent opportunity for outdoor adventures. Plan a day trip to Balea Lake, where you can take a scenic cable car ride up to the Capra Chalet for unparalleled mountain views. Alternatively, tackle the expansive walking trails of Dumbrava Sibiului Natural Park or Paltinis Ski Resort for a rejuvenating escape from city life.

After working up an appetite on your adventures, indulge in some scrumptious Romanian cuisine at any number of excellent local eateries. Savor traditional dishes such as "sarmale" (stuffed cabbage rolls) or "mamaliga" (polenta with cheese), each offering phenomenal bursts of flavor that entice even the most discerning palate.

Sibiu—a captivating city brimming with charm and wonder—awaits those who yearn for fresh experiences and unforgettable memories. Discover its rich history, wander through its picturesque streetscapes or explore its lush surroundings. You'll uncover why Sibiu is a must-visit destination on your next European adventure.

Plovdiv, Bulgaria

Plovdiv, the hidden gem of Bulgaria, is one of the oldest cities in Europe. With its rich history, vibrant culture, and breathtaking landscapes, this city promises a one-of-a-kind experience for avid travelers.

Nestled between seven hills along the banks of the Maritsa River, Plovdiv is famous for its ancient Roman architecture, colorful streets, and lively art scene. As you begin to explore the city, you'll find that every corner presents a fascinating blend of old-world charm and modern vibrancy.

One of Plovdiv's most popular attractions is the Ancient Theatre, dating back to the 1st century AD. This remarkably preserved amphitheater still hosts performances today, allowing visitors to experience art and entertainment within its ancient walls. While in Plovdiv, be sure not to miss a show here; it's a once-in-a-lifetime opportunity!

Another significant historical site worth visiting is the Roman Odeon. Constructed during Emperor Trajan's rule, this archaeological wonder is smaller than the more famous Ancient Theatre but offers a close-up look at exquisite mosaic floors and well-preserved ruins.

As you wander through Plovdiv's Old Town, pay a visit to the stunning St. Constantine and Helena Church. This impressive Eastern Orthodox Church showcases ornate frescoes on its walls and ceilings that will leave you awestruck. The church itself is an emblem of Bulgaria's rich religious heritage.

For adventurous travelers who enjoy outdoor activities, don't miss out on hiking around one of Plovdiv's surrounding hills: Nebet Tepe. From its peak, you'll be rewarded with panoramic views of the entire city – an ideal spot for photographers.

Art lovers should definitely check out Kapana - Plovdiv's creative district. In recent years, this area has transformed into a bustling hub for artists and musicians, featuring contemporary galleries, street art, and lively cafes.

No visit to Plovdiv would be complete without immersing yourself in Bulgarian cuisine. Sample delicious traditional dishes such as kavarma, banitsa, or shopska salad at one of the city's many cozy restaurants or family-owned establishments. Don't forget to pair your meal with a lovely local wine – Plovdiv is known for its excellent wineries!

To gain insight into Plovdiv's past, head over to the Regional Ethnographic Museum. Housed in a beautifully restored 19th-century house, this museum exhibits traditional clothing, crafts, and furniture that provide a glimpse into the daily life of Bulgarians from centuries ago.

Finally, take the time to embrace the vibrant nightlife Plovdiv offers. Whether you're looking to dance the night away at a lively nightclub or simply enjoy a relaxing evening at a jazz cafe, the city has something for everyone.

In conclusion, Plovdiv should be on every traveler's bucket list. With its rich history seamlessly interwoven with modern culture and art, traveling to this Bulgarian marvel promises memories that will last a lifetime. Don't miss out on this incredible opportunity to immerse yourself in the beauty and allure of Plovdiv – pack your bags and book your flights today!

Scandinavian Europe

Visby Sweden

Visby, a picturesque town on the island of Gotland, Sweden, is a true hidden gem for travelers looking to experience the charm of medieval Europe. This UNESCO World Heritage site is renowned for its impeccably preserved medieval architecture and enchanting cobblestone streets lined with charming shops, cafes, and historical landmarks. Visiting Visby is akin to stepping back in time, as the city's 13th-century walls encircle the old town, beckoning history enthusiasts and wanderlust-filled souls.

Getting to Visby is surprisingly simple, considering its location on an island in the Baltic Sea. Gotland's airport connects to major Swedish cities such as Stockholm and Gothenburg with daily flights operated by regional airlines. Alternatively, ferries run regularly from Nynäshamn and Oskarshamn on the mainland to Visby's modern port.

Once you arrive in Visby, it's impossible not to be captivated by the city's vibrant atmosphere. The well-preserved city walls, known as Ringmuren or The Ring Wall, provide a striking backdrop as 27 of the original 29 watchtowers still stand proudly around the medieval town. These walls not only encapsulate history but also serve as a testament to the craftsmanship of a bygone era.

Visby's old town comprises quaint houses adorned with blooming flowers in summer and colorful foliage in autumn. Meandering along these narrow cobblestoned paths will lead you past numerous historical landmarks, including ruins of once-famous churches like St. Nicolai and St. Karin.

St. Mary's Cathedral or Sankta Maria Kyrka is an architectural marvel that embodies both Gothic and Romanesque styles. Its construction commenced in the 12th century and underwent multiple expansions over time. The cathedral remains an active house of worship while also housing a small museum showcasing ecclesiastical artifacts.

One of Visby's most iconic ruins is undoubtedly the Visby Sankt Olof or St. Olof Church's remnants, dating back to the 13th century. A formidable watchtower now accompanies these hauntingly beautiful ruins, offering unparalleled views of the city and the coast.

Visitors cannot miss the unmistakable sight of the Powder Tower (Kruttornet) – thought to be Visby's oldest surviving tower – perched on a hill near the waterfront. This fortification dates back to the 12th century and has an uncertain history but played a significant role in defending the town.

To truly immerse yourself in Gotland's history and culture, plan your visit during one of Visby's annual events. The Medieval Week showcases Nordic medieval history through authentic costumes, reenactments, and entertaining performances. Similarly, Almedalen Week brings together politicians, academics, and journalists for Sweden's largest political event.

Visby offers a diverse culinary scene that features local flavors and international dishes. Savor a taste of Gotland with traditional specialties such as saffranspannkaka (saffron pancake) or indulge in fresh seafood dishes made from catches brought straight from the Baltic Sea.

Several cafes or "Fikas" offer respite after a long day exploring the city with coffee and local pastries.

Visby accommodation options cater to every budget and preference, ranging from charming guesthouses nestled within cozy alleys to luxurious modern hotels offering stunning sea views.

In conclusion, a trip to Visby presents a unique opportunity to explore a beautifully preserved medieval city teeming with history, architecture, and enchanting natural beauty. Whether you are a fan of historical wonders or simply seeking picturesque landscapes, Visby is a destination that shouldn't be missed when visiting Sweden.

Viborg , Denmark

Nestled in the heart of Jutland Peninsula, Viborg serves as a picturesque reminder of Denmark's medieval era. With its cobbled streets, timber-framed buildings and charming atmosphere, it has become an increasingly sought-after destination for travelers seeking authentic Danish experiences. This idyllic city boasts alluring natural landscapes, rich history and culture, and exceptional opportunities for exploration. In this article, we'll delve into the unique attractions that make Viborg worth your visit.

As you walk through the city, you'll come across pristine architectural marvels that provide glimpses into Viborg's heritage. The city is synonymous with its iconic cathedral - Viborg Domkirke - a beautiful example of Romanesque-

Lutheran architecture. The twin towers dominate the skyline, while the intricately decorated interior showcases medieval frescoes depicting biblical stories.

Wander through Latinerhaven, a historic Latin Quarter that showcases half-timbered houses and boutique shops lining cobbled streets. Pay a visit to Toldboden - awash with colorful Danish buildings steeped in history; it's an embodiment of Scandinavian atmosphere and aesthetic.

To witness Denmark's natural beauty at its finest, look no further than Hald Sø Lake and Dollerup Bakker hills. Located just south of Viborg city center, this area offers an enchanting landscape teeming with flora and fauna.

Embark on a peaceful stroll or bike ride around Hald Sø to soak in panoramas overlooking the lake. For avid birdwatchers, there are several observation points that provide excellent opportunities to spot various bird species nesting in local marshes.

Dollerup Bakker is a sprawling mosaic of dense woodlands and heath-covered slopes offering scenic hiking trails. This nature reserve is popular for invigorating walks, trail running, and outdoor picnics in the rolling hills.

The Viborg Museum tells the story of this ancient city with a vast collection of exhibits depicting periods from the Stone Age to present day. Marvel at historical artifacts, art pieces, and photographs that showcase the area's changing landscape, commerce, and everyday life.

This museum also houses temporary exhibitions focusing on different aspects of Viborg's heritage or showcasing local artists' works. It's an immersive cultural experience that any history buff should not miss.

Situated within an old Renaissance building near Viborg Cathedral, Skovgaard Museum is dedicated to Danish art and its contribution to Scandinavia's cultural essence. A must-visit for art enthusiasts, this museum proudly exhibits the Skovgaard family's masterpieces – an artistic dynasty that spans three generations.

The museum also features works from other acclaimed artists such as Joakim Skovgaard and his eminent frescoes depicting ancient Nordic mythology.

Borgvold Park is an oasis of serenity amid the bustling city center—a perfect spot to unwind after a day of exploration. With romantically sculpted gardens, picturesque ponds and flower beds in full bloom during summers, Borgvold Park mirrors a fairy tale setting.

Relish delightful Danish pastries and coffee at one of the park cafés or bring your own picnic basket to embrace true hygge – the practice of appreciating simple comforts.

Viborg is a haven for history enthusiasts, nature lovers, art aficionados, and those looking for an authentic Danish experience. It's a charming reminder that Denmark has much more to offer than Copenhagen, and that there are numerous destinations in Denmark that are worth exploring.

Porvoo, Finland

Nestled along the beautiful Porvoonjoki River, Porvoo is an enchanting Finnish town brimming with history and charm. Home to Finland's second oldest town, dating back to the 14th century, this idyllic destination offers visitors a fascinating blend of maritime culture, wooden architecture and mouthwatering cuisine. Just a 50-kilometer drive east of Helsinki, Porvoo serves as a perfect day trip for travelers looking to experience the quieter side of Finland.

The first thing one notices upon arrival in Porvoo is its iconic red wooden-arched houses lining the riverfront – an area known as Old Porvoo. Originally painted red in honor of King Gustav III of Sweden's visit in 1760, these delightful houses create a picturesque landscape that has become synonymous with the town, drawing tourists from around the world.

Stroll along its cobbled streets and immerse yourself in centuries-old history and architectural marvels. Among the many attractions in Old Porvoo is its medieval cathedral built in the 15th century, an enduring symbol dedicated to Saint Mary. Visit this awe-inspiring stone church and marvel at its simplicity; inside you'll find wooden galleries exemplifying Nordic craftsmanship.

Porvoo's links to iconic Finnish literature are unmistakable. Tourists can explore major sights connected to Finland's national writer Johan Ludvig Runeberg. The Runeberg House stands testament to his life and work; it also doubles up as a museum where visitors can view memorabilia from Runeberg's life. Satisfy your sweet tooth by trying the delicious

Runeberg's tart, a delicacy invented by Runeberg's wife Fredrika and still being sold today in local bakeries.

Gastronomy is an inseparable part of any vacation, and Porvoo does not disappoint. The town has recently emerged as a gastronomic hotspot, with many restaurants showcasing delicious, locally-sourced Finnish dishes. Do not leave without experiencing the local cuisine at places like Bistro Gustaf and Zum Beispiel, which offer unique fusion menus combining traditional Finnish ingredients with international culinary trends. For a truly authentic experience, Johan's – a restaurant housed in a 19th-century building – serves up typical coastal dishes using seasonal ingredients.

In addition to its rich history, natural beauty is woven into Porvoo's fabric. The surrounding forests, lakes and waterways are sure to enthrall outdoor enthusiasts. Canoeing along the Porvoonjoki River is an immersive way to discover the pristine nature that borders the town. Those seeking solace can go for long hikes or bike rides across myriad nature trails in the area. In winter months, cross-country skiing is also possible through snow-laden landscapes offering panoramic views of the majestic Finnish wilderness.

For lovers of art and handicrafts, Porvoo proves to be an inspiring destination. Admire local craftsmanship at small shops and boutiques selling ceramics, jewelry and glass art that embody unique Nordic designs. The nearby Pellavaa & Piikkolaa Art House showcases contemporary Finnish artists, while the Oura Glass Factory allows visitors to observe glassblowers in action.

Porvoo is not just a destination; it is an experience captivating all the senses and leaving an indelible imprint on your memory. Discover this quaint maritime town where history, culture, picturesque landscapes and delectable cuisine come together to create the ideal Finnish getaway.

Siglufjordur, Iceland

Siglufjordur, a hidden gem tucked away in North Iceland, is an enchanting coastal village that captivates the hearts of tourists and adventurers. With its stunning landscapes, colorful homes, and a vibrant culture rooted in the history of herring fishing, Siglufjordur offers visitors an unforgettable experience. In this article, we will explore the various attractions and activities you can indulge in while discovering the alluring beauty of Siglufjordur.

Known for its picturesque scenery, Siglufjordur is surrounded by magnificent snow-capped mountains that embrace the serene fjord below. One of the most rewarding ways to appreciate this breathtaking view is by venturing on one of the many hiking trails around the area. The Strákar hiking path is a popular choice as it presents a moderate challenge that caters to both amateurs and experienced hikers alike while offering panoramic views of the town and its surroundings.

A visit to Siglufjordur wouldn't be complete without learning about its rich history as a thriving herring fishing center from the early 1900s to 1970s. The Herring Era

Museum is an award-winning museum which features exhibitions about Icelandic herring fisheries, its economic and social impact on the country, as well as showcasing various artifacts and restored fishing boats that were used during this prosperous era. Delve into this bygone era that shaped Iceland's growth through immersive and interactive displays at this fascinating museum.

Another iconic cultural attraction in Siglufjordur is the Rauðka Café-Museum-Dairy Farm combo. This unique establishment consists of three elements: a cozy café, a small dairy farm where visitors can see traditional Icelandic skyr being made, and a modern art gallery featuring local artists' creations. With its friendly and warm atmosphere, Rauðka is an ideal place to enjoy a cup of coffee while savoring the local art and culture.

Siglufjordur is also a winter wonderland, especially for skiing and snowboarding enthusiasts. Numerous skiing trails are scattered across the mountains, ranging from beginner slopes to more challenging terrain for experienced skiers. The town's ski resort, Skarðsdalur, is known for its well-maintained trails and an idyllic location that overlooks the fjord. The resort also offers quality ski equipment rentals and lessons for visitors who wish to explore these snowy slopes.

For those seeking a more relaxing experience amidst Siglufjordur's stunning landscapes, embark on a boat tour around the fjord. These tours are led by experienced local skippers who narrate fascinating stories about the town's history and folklore while cruising through the calm waters. Enjoy a unique perspective of the village as you explore hidden coves teeming with wildlife and sail past towering cliffs cascading into the sea.

Finally, cap off your Siglufjordur adventure with a visit to the charming Hannes Boy Café located at the harbor. This popular eatery has been buzzing with tourists and locals since 1975 and offers a variety of delicious Icelandic dishes made with fresh, locally sourced ingredients - including tender lamb chops, perfectly cooked arctic char, and flavorful homemade bread.

In conclusion, Siglufjordur truly captures the essence of Iceland's pristine beauty and rich cultural heritage. With its mesmerizing landscapes, invigorating outdoor activities, and enthralling museums showcasing unparalleled local history - this enchanting coastal village leaves visitors longing for more. So pack your bags and embark on an extraordinary journey to discover the magical realm of Siglufjordur, Iceland!

Bergen, Norway

Situated between the majestic fjords and the awe-inspiring mountains, Bergen, Norway is a city where nature and culture collide. Known as the Gateway to the Fjords, this vibrant coastal town boasts rich maritime history and some of the most iconic Norwegian landscapes.

Bergen is easily accessible by plane, train, or ferry. The city's international airport, Bergen Airport Flesland, welcomes flights from many European cities.

Alternatively, you can take a picturesque train ride from Oslo or board a scenic Hurtigruten cruise along Norway's western coast.

Once in Bergen, public transportation options include buses, trams, and taxis. The compact city center is also ideal for exploring on foot or by bike.

Bergen offers a plethora of historic sites, museums, and outdoor activities. One must-visit location is Bryggen – a UNESCO World Heritage Site featuring colorful wooden buildings that date back to the Hanseatic era. Stroll along the narrow alleyways and peek into charming shops selling traditional Norwegian goods.

Another cultural highlight is the KODE Art Museums and Composer Homes, which houses an extensive collection of works by legendary Norwegian artist Edvard Munch. Additionally, music lovers won't want to miss visiting Edvard Grieg's picturesque home at Troldhaugen.

For stunning views of Bergen and its surrounding fjords, board the Fløibanen funicular that transports you up Mount Fløyen. At the summit, you can enjoy numerous hiking trails or simply relax at the panoramic café while soaking in mesmerizing vistas. To take your love for nature a step further, embark on a fjord cruise or join a guided kayak tour, where you can marvel at steep cliffs and cascading waterfalls up close.

Bergen's culinary scene should not be overlooked. Fresh seafood can be found in abundance, particularly at the lively Fish Market, where you can sample local delicacies like fish soup and freshly-shucked oysters. For a more upscale dining experience, head to Lysverket or Bare Vestland to savor contemporary Nordic cuisine.

The city's nightlife offers a range of options as well. Groups looking for a cozy atmosphere can visit one of Bergen's many microbreweries, while those seeking an energetic night out should venture to Hulen, a unique club located inside a cave!

Bergen caters to all travelers with accommodations ranging from budget-friendly hostels to luxurious hotels. For a memorable stay, consider the historic Opus XVI or the eclectic Magic Hotel on Korskirken square.

As for budgeting, keep in mind that Norway can be expensive for tourists. Plan your activities accordingly and make use of local supermarkets and free attractions to maximize your savings.

Bergen is a year-round destination with each season offering distinctive charms. Summer (June-August) welcomes long days, pleasant temperatures, and blooming landscapes – ideal for outdoor activities. Autumn (September-October) is perfect for witnessing vibrant foliage and fewer crowds. Winter (November-February) invites snow enthusiasts for skiing and ice climbing adventures, while spring (March-May) ushers in budding nature trails and milder weather conditions.

Bergen offers an enriching experience for any traveler seeking an idyllic blend of history, culture, and breathtaking nature. Start planning your Norwegian adventure today – the fjords are calling!

Uppsala, Sweden

Located about an hour north of Stockholm, the bustling city of Uppsala is steeped in history, natural beauty, and unique cultural experiences. This Swedish gem boasts picturesque landscapes, ancient Old Town quarters, and a rich intellectual legacy anchored by its prestigious university. A visit to Uppsala will surely leave you captivated by its charming atmosphere and unforgettable sights.

Upon arriving in Uppsala, it is impossible not to notice the dominating presence of the Uppsala Cathedral. The tallest church in Scandinavia exudes a sense of awe and wonder through its towering spires and impressive Gothic architecture. Inside, visitors have a chance to admire stunning frescoes, elaborate altar decorations, and learn about Sweden's rich history through various ecclesiastical relics. The cathedral is also the final resting place for several Swedish kings and important figures.

Next to the cathedral lies another testament to Uppsala's illustrious past – the Gustavianum Museum. This majestic building houses an extensive collection of artifacts from Sweden's pre-Viking age to its modern era. The Augsburg Art Cabinet and the Anatomical Theatre are highlights within the museum that offer insights into various aspects–from artistry to scientific discoveries–that shaped Sweden throughout the centuries.

The spirit of academia runs strong in this lively city; not just because of prominent institutions like Uppsala University but also because of Carolina Rediviva, Northern Europe's oldest university library. With more than 5 million books and countless manuscripts dating back centuries, it will fascinate both scholars and laypeople alike.

Immerse yourself in Swedish culture by exploring the Gamla (Old) Uppsala region. This historic area is home to royal burial mounds that date back to the 6th century as well as an open-air museum showcasing ancient Nordic buildings immersed atop beautiful meadows filled with flowers. Visitors should not miss the Disagården Open-Air Museum, which provides a glimpse into the traditional Swedish way of life during the 19th century.

Nature enthusiasts will love the Uppsala Botanical Gardens situated near the tranquil waters of Fyris River. The verdant oasis encompasses more than 11,000 plant species and features a marvelous Baroque garden that doubles as an outdoor exhibition space during the summer. While there, also take time to visit the Linnaeus Museum and Gardens, dedicated to the world-renowned botanist Carl Linnaeus. Here, you can surround yourself with blooming splendor and learn about his contributions to natural science.

Uppsala's culinary scene is nothing short of delicious either. Sample unique Nordic flavors at various local eateries that use fresh ingredients and traditional methods to create modern Swedish cuisine. Don't forget to indulge in some fika – coffee breaks accompanied by tasty pastries – while you're in town.

Lastly, one must not leave Uppsala without experiencing its lively nightlife scene. Fueled by a predominantly young population, Uppsala offers a diverse selection of bars, clubs, and pubs where visitors can unwind and enjoy their evenings just as Swedes do.

Uppsala holds a charm that is unmistakably unique yet unmistakably Swedish at the same time. Offering visitors an exceptional mix of history, culture, nature, and vibrant city life – exploring this enchanting city should be at the top of any traveler's bucket list.

Lofoten Islands, Norway

Traveling to the majestic Lofoten Islands in Norway is an experience you will not easily forget. Known for its dramatic landscapes and quaint fishing villages, this enchanting archipelago offers an unforgettable journey full of breathtaking natural beauty, rich history, and exciting outdoor adventures.

Upon arrival, your senses are immediately awakened by the spectacular vistas on display. Majestic mountains seem to rise out of the icy waters, reflecting their awe-inspiring peaks in the still fjords below. As you explore this mesmerizing landscape, the song of seabirds fills the air, and the scent of Arctic flora envelops your surroundings.

One of Lofoten's most distinctive features is its distinctive fishing villages that are scattered along the coasts. The iconic red wooden cabins called Rorbu can be found dotting the shoreline. These traditional fishermen's huts were once the seasonal homes for those who ventured to these isles to capitalize on the abundant fish stocks. Today, Rorbu has been transformed into cozy guest accommodations that allow visitors a glimpse into Lofoten's rich seafaring heritage while providing a comfortable base from which to explore the islands.

No visit to Lofoten would be complete without immersing yourself in its vibrant culture and fascinating history. Travelers can visit local museums that tell tales of Viking exploration and document the area's fishing legacy. Plus, don't miss out on experiencing a traditional Norwegian meal prepared using fresh, seasonal ingredients straight from land or sea.

If you crave adventure, the Lofoten Islands offer ample opportunity for hiking, climbing, and exploring. For hikers, there are well-marked trails that cater to all levels of fitness and skill. You can challenge yourself with steep mountain treks or enjoy leisurely strolls through pristine forests and along stunning coastal paths. With midnight sun in summer or Northern Lights in winter as your backdrop, each step you take introduces new wonders.

For avid climbers, Lofoten provides a unique and compelling playground that boasts some impressive granite walls and rock formations. There's no shortage of climbing routes that cater to beginners and skilled climbers alike. Connected to the mainland by a series of bridges, these islands also offer the opportunity for scenic road trips or cycle tours along winding coastal roads and through vibrant green pastures.

For water enthusiasts, the Lofoten Islands are home to world-class surfing conditions. Brave the crystal clear waves amidst picturesque settings of snow-capped peaks, remote beaches, and verdant forests. For those seeking underwater expeditions, the area's diverse marine life and clear waters make snorkeling or diving here an unmissable experience.

If relaxation is more your style, there are plenty of serene spots to unwind and soak in the islands' captivating beauty. Stroll along pristine white sand beaches while enjoying panoramic views of turquoise waters and soaring cliffs. Or take a leisurely boat trip around the archipelago - witness stunning sea eagles soar overhead, encounter playful otters in their natural habitat, or spot schools of fish leaping gracefully from the depths.

When night falls in Lofoten, be prepared for a real treat if you're visiting during the winter months. As darkness envelops this Arctic paradise, watch the sky erupt into a mesmerizing display of colors as the Northern Lights dance above you.

A journey to the remote yet breathtakingly beautiful Lofoten Islands allows visitors to uncover the magic that exists within this unique corner of Norway. Offering once in a lifetime experiences amidst a stunning natural landscape steeped in rich history and culture, there's no doubt that this enchanting destination will leave you with memories you'll cherish forever.

Aarhus, Denmark

Aarhus, Denmark, a charming coastal city located on the eastern side of the Jutland Peninsula, has become an increasingly popular destination for travelers seeking a blend of modern culture, history, and natural beauty. With its picturesque waterfront setting, vibrant culinary scene, and mix of architectural styles, Aarhus offers visitors a memorable and enriching travel experience.

Arriving in Aarhus is relatively simple by various means of transportation. Its well-connected international airport welcomes flights from numerous European cities, while the train system connects Aarhus to Copenhagen and other regional destinations. Travelers can also drive to the city or take advantage of the multiple ferry connections from destinaions across Scandinavia.

One of the most prominent landmarks in Aarhus is the ARoS Art Museum. This unique museum features an intriguing circular walkway known as "Your rainbow panorama," showcasing contemporary art with a touch of magic. The mesmerizing colorful glass installation appeals to visitors of all ages and provides stunning views of the city below.

History enthusiasts will appreciate Den Gamle By (The Old Town). This open-air living history museum allows visitors to journey back in time through authentic reconstructions of Danish homes and historic buildings from various periods throughout the last five centuries. From blacksmith shops to bakeries, Den Gamle By captures the essence of Danish life from days gone by.

Another important attraction is Aarhus Cathedral. As one of the longest and tallest churches in Denmark, this cathedral is not only an architectural marvel but also home to significant religious artifacts and exquisite frescoes that date back to the 15th century.

For nature lovers, Aarhus offers plenty to explore as well. The serene Botanical Gardens encompass over 50 acres and showcase a variety of local plant species alongside more exotic fauna in several greenhouses. Moreover, just a short distance from the city center lies Risskov Forest - perfect for invigorating walks or bike rides while appreciating the natural beauty surrounding Aarhus.

One of the must-see events in Aarhus is the annual Aarhus Food Festival, drawing food enthusiasts worldwide with its innovative approach to Nordic cuisine. Travelers can also indulge in New Nordic gastronomy year-round at various restaurants and cafes spread throughout the city. Traditional Danish dishes mingle with modern culinary creativity, encouraging visitors to sample new flavors and delight their taste buds.

For travelers who wish to explore more of Denmark's history, the Moesgaard Museum is another gem located just outside Aarhus' city limits. This stunningly modern museum features incredible archaeological finds and focuses on Danish prehistory and ancient civilizations. The internationally renowned exhibitions incorporate immersive elements to showcase a fascinating array of artifacts.

A wander through the charming Latin Quarter offers travelers a maze of narrow, cobblestone streets lined with colorful houses, chic boutiques, galleries, bars, and cafes. This hip neighborhood provides plenty of opportunities for shopping, dining, or relaxing with a cup of coffee as you watch the world pass by.

Aarhus, Denmark guarantees an unforgettable experience filled with vibrant culture, rich history, and alluring natural beauty. With its welcoming atmosphere paired with noteworthy attractions and enjoyable activities, Aarhus is an ideal destination for both relaxation and adventure seeking travelers looking for an enchanting coastal getaway.

Oulu, Finland

Oulu, a fascinating city located in the Northern Ostrobothnia region of Finland, is a travel destination that offers both natural and urban experiences unlike any other. With its rich history, diverse attractions, and stunning landscapes, Oulu has captured the hearts of many who venture to this northern paradise.

The journey to Oulu can be an adventure in itself. Whether arriving by plane from Helsinki or taking the scenic train ride through the Finnish countryside, travelers are greeted with spectacular vistas as they make their way to this captivating city. As the landscape transforms from lush forests to frozen tundras during winter months, visitors get a glimpse at the true beauty and mystique of life in the Arctic Circle.

Upon arriving in Oulu, it is apparent that this city seamlessly blends tradition with modernity. Ancient buildings share streets with contemporary structures, creating an ambiance that is uniquely Oulu. Exploring its historic district is an essential part of visiting this enchanting city. One of Oulu's most notable landmarks is the 19th-century Cathedral, an imposing white structure that boasts intricate wooden carvings and a rich history.

For nature enthusiasts, Oulu offers numerous parks and green spaces where leisurely strolls or cycling adventures can be enjoyed. Hupisaaret Islands Park is a picturesque haven that lies within Oulujoki River estuary – an oasis of tranquility and respite amidst the bustling cityscape. With its interconnected waterways and charming bridges scattered throughout the park, Hupisaaret provides the perfect setting for immersing oneself in Finland's natural beauty.

Oulu's coastal location also presents endless opportunities for water-based activities. Nallikari Beach is a popular spot where locals and tourists alike revel in the sun-kissed sand dunes during summer months. For a more exhilarating experience, brave souls can plunge into the icy waters at Tuira Beach – an unforgettable dip that's sure to invigorate the senses.

When seeking an authentic taste of Finland, Oulu's diverse culinary scene does not disappoint. Local delicacies like reindeer, vendace, and kalakukko (a traditional fish pie) can be found in several restaurants throughout the city. Stopping at local cafes to indulge in Finnish pastries like korvapuusti (cinnamon roll) and pulla (sweet cardamom bread) is an essential part of any Oulu trip.

One cannot visit Oulu without embracing the city's thriving cultural milieu. The city offers various museums, galleries, and theaters that showcase the richness and diversity of Finnish artistry. A visit to Oulu Art Museum or an evening spent enjoying performances at Madetoja Concert Hall gives travelers a stronger appreciation for the creativity that stems from this northern haven.

During winter months, Oulu transforms into a magical snow-covered wonderland. Auroras illuminate the night sky creating a display of colors that captivate both locals and visitors. Winter sports enthusiasts flock to Oulu to embark on arctic adventures such as cross-country skiing, snowshoeing, and ice fishing.

Oulu's lively market square is the pulse of life in this vibrant community. The marketplace bustles with activity as vendors sell fresh produce, handcrafted items, and culinary delights all year long. In addition to shopping for souvenirs or sampling Finnish cuisine, the market square is an ideal location for socializing and embracing the warmth of the local community.

Combining natural splendors with stimulating urban experiences, traveling to Oulu creates memories that will last a lifetime. From exploring its historic treasures to basking in its untamed beauty, a trip to Oulu reveals why this gem in Northern Finland remains undeniably mesmerizing.

Torshavn, Faroe Islands

Traveling to the picturesque town of Torshavn, the capital city of the Faroe Islands, is an experience that will transport you to a world away from the hustle and bustle of everyday life. Nestled amidst dramatic landscapes and rugged coastline, Torshavn is a charming destination that offers a perfect blend of natural beauty, history, and culture.

As your plane descends into Vágar Airport, you will be greeted with breathtaking views of the surrounding mountains and the vast expanse of North Atlantic Ocean. From there, it's a one-hour drive to Torshavn. However, it is important to note that one can also reach the city by ferry or helicopter depending on your preference and budget.

On your journey to Torshavn, you will be captivated by the stunning vistas unfolding before your eyes; a mosaic of quaint villages perched atop vertiginous cliffs, emerald-green valley floors carpeted with velvety grass, and tumbling waterfalls cascading down from lofty peaks.

Upon arriving in Torshavn, you will instantly feel its intimate atmosphere and welcoming ambiance. The town is best explored on foot, meandering through its maze-like lanes that wind through a labyrinth of colorful turf-roofed houses. The Old Town or Tínganes is undoubtedly the heart of Torshavn, boasting one of Northern Europe's oldest parliamentary meeting places, dating back more than a thousand years.

The rich history of the Faroese people can also be uncovered at the National Museum in Torshavn where relics dating back to Viking times are preserved. In addition, several art galleries specializing in Faroese art are dotted around the town showcasing local talents.

Food lovers will rejoice at the array of dining options available in Torshavn. The culinary scene boasts flavors infused with fresh local produce including seafood caught straight from surrounding waters. From upscale fine-dining establishments to cozy cafes offering traditional homemade dishes like fish balls and fermented lamb, there is something to satiate every appetite.

Accompanying the sublime gastronomical experiences are the local tipple favorites of akvavit and brennevín alongside traditional Faroese beer. Numerous pubs and bars in town offer live music, making them perfect places to unwind after a day of exploring.

The striking landscapes and remote setting of the Faroe Islands have inspired a rich tradition of woolen products, particularly hand-knit sweaters with distinctive patterns. A trip to Torshavn is incomplete without browsing through these exquisite crafts in local shops. Moreover, the town also hosts an annual cultural event called Olavsøka, a celebration of Faroese identity, with parades, music, sports events, and more.

Torshavn serves as an excellent base to explore some of the 18 mesmerizing islands that make up the Faroe Islands archipelago. Take advantage of guided tours that offer hikes to isolated corners where you can witness majestic seabird colonies or sail on boats drifting between towering cliffs. Opportunities for kayaking, diving, bird-watching, and horse riding are also aplenty for outdoor enthusiasts.

Traveling to Torshavn is an unforgettable adventure overflowing with history, culture, gastronomy, and astonishing natural panoramas. Its allure emanates from its unspoiled landscapes and laid-back character that provides a much-needed reprieve from fast-paced city life. So pack your bags for an experience of a lifetime in this treasure trove tucked away in the North Atlantic Ocean.

Travel Tips for Off the Beaten Path Adventures

Navigating Different Transportation Options

Europe is a treasure trove of hidden gems that offer unique experiences for intrepid travelers. When it comes to exploring off-the-beaten-path destinations in Europe, there are many travel tips to keep in mind. One crucial aspect is navigating different transportation options available, as it can be overwhelming and sometimes challenging. Here are some practical suggestions to help you traverse the lesser-known regions of Europe with ease.

Research transportation options beforehand

Before setting off on your adventure, be sure to research the best ways to reach your obscure destination. Some areas might only be accessible by car, while others can only be reached by public transport or via specific routes. Consult regional guidebooks, online forums, and travel blogs for advice on the most effective routes to take.

Use trains as your main mode of transport

Train travel is one of the most convenient ways to explore lesser-known areas in Europe. Regional trains connect major cities with remote locations and often provide affordable and scenic journeys. To save time and money, consider buying a Eurail pass or investigate regional passes that cater to specific areas of interest.

Be prepared to utilize buses and minibuses

In many rural areas across Europe, buses and minibuses serve as essential modes of transportation – even where train lines do not extend. Bus services are generally reliable and can be a more economical option when compared to trains or private transportation methods.

Hitchhiking is an option but use caution

Hitchhiking is not uncommon in some parts of Europe; however, we recommend researching safety guidelines and being aware of local customs before deciding on this mode of transport. Always trust your instincts when seeking a ride from strangers, and never venture alone.

Renting a car offers flexibility

Renting a car gives you the freedom to chart your own course through the countryside, explore off-the-beaten-path destinations, and stop whenever you please. Keep in mind that different countries may have unique driving laws and regulations, and some may even require you to obtain an international driver's license – familiarize yourself with local rules before hitting the road.

Remember to book your car rentals in advance to secure favorable rates.

Biking is environmentally friendly and fun

Cycling is an excellent way to explore lesser-known areas while also being environmentally friendly. Many European countries have well-developed cycling infrastructure, making it a practical option for travelers seeking off-the-beaten-path experiences. Research suitable routes, pack necessities such as puncture repair kits and helmets, and you're good to go.

Consider carpooling or shared rides

Carpooling with friends or using shared ride services like BlaBlaCar can be an enjoyable and cost-effective way of exploring Europe's hidden corners. Not only do you save money on transportation costs, but you also get to meet new people and hear their travel stories.

Embrace local transportation

In some places, there might be unconventional means of transportation – such as donkey carts or cable cars – which provide a unique experience and help immerse you in the local culture. Don't shy away from these opportunities if they arise; it could turn into a memorable story.

Prepare for challenges

Transportation in off the grid areas can be infrequent or limited in service. It's crucial to exercise patience and remain adaptable when delays arise or when conditions are not ideal.

By considering these travel tips for navigating different transportation options, you're well-equipped to embark on an unforgettable off-the-beaten-path adventure through Europe's hidden gems.

Conclusion

Hidden Europe - Small cities and towns that are off the beaten path, has taken readers on a charming and insightful journey through some of the lesser-known gems of Europe. These enchanting locations, each with their unique histories, cultures, and landscapes, offer a refreshing alternative to the well-trodden tourist spots that have become all too familiar.

As we ventured through the winding roads of these hidden destinations, we discovered the rich tapestry of European heritage woven together by centuries of interconnected histories. From medieval castles perched atop picturesque hills to vibrant local markets brimming with regional delicacies, these small cities and towns have opened up a world both magical and undiscovered.

Furthermore, our journey emphasized the importance of responsible tourism and preservation. By traveling off the beaten path and engaging with these communities authentically, we can contribute to their sustainability and support their local economies. This approach ensures that these hidden gems retain their charm for generations to come.

Lastly, we hope that this book has not only inspired readers to seek out new adventures but has also cultivated a deeper appreciation for Europe's cultural riches. These quaint cities and towns serve as a reminder that there is much more to discover beyond what initially meets the eye, as long as one remains open to exploration.

So pack your bags and set off on your journey to uncover these hidden treasures – immerse yourself in the world of Hidden Europe, where awe-inspiring stories and unforgettable experiences await in every corner.

Printed in Great Britain
by Amazon

91cad975-7b02-41b2-b475-d097951a0d26R01